Teaching the Developmental Education Student

Kenneth M. Ahrendt, *Editor*
Oregon State University

NEW DIRECTIONS FOR COMMUNITY COLLEGES
ARTHUR M. COHEN, *Editor-in-Chief*
FLORENCE B. BRAWER, *Associate Editor*

Number 57, Spring 1987

Paperback sourcebooks in
The Jossey-Bass Higher Education Series

Jossey-Bass Inc., Publishers
San Francisco • London

EDUCATIONAL RESOURCES INFORMATION CENTER

Clearinghouse For Junior Colleges

UNIVERSITY OF CALIFORNIA, LOS ANGELES

Kenneth M. Ahrendt (ed.).
Teaching the Developmental Education Student.
New Directions for Community Colleges, no. 57.
Volume XV, number 1.
San Francisco: Jossey-Bass, 1987.

New Directions for Community Colleges
Arthur M. Cohen, *Editor-in-Chief;* Florence B. Brawer, *Associate Editor*

New Directions for Community Colleges is published quarterly by Jossey-Bass
Inc., Publishers (publication number USPS 121-710), in association with the
ERIC Clearinghouse for Junior Colleges. *New Directions* is numbered
sequentially—please order extra copies by sequential number. The volume and
issue numbers above are included for the convenience of libraries. Second-class
postage paid at San Francisco, California, and at additional mailing offices.
POSTMASTER: Send address changes to Jossey-Bass, Inc., Publishers,
433 California Street, San Francisco, California 94104.

The material in this publication was prepared pursuant to a contract with
the Office of Educational Research and Improvement, U.S. Department of
Education. Contractors undertaking such projects under government sponsorship
are encouraged to express freely their judgment in professional and technical
matters. Prior to publication, the manuscript was submitted to the Center for
the Study of Community Colleges for critical review and determination of
professional competence. This publication has met such standards. Points of
view or opinions, however, do not necessarily represent the official view or
opinions of the Center for the Study of Community Colleges or the Office
of Educational Research and Improvement.

Editorial correspondence should be sent to the Editor-in-Chief, Arthur M. Cohen,
at the ERIC Clearinghouse for Junior Colleges, University of California,
Los Angeles, California 90024.

Library of Congress Catalog Card Number LC 85-644753

International Standard Serial Number ISSN 0194-3081

International Standard Book Number ISBN 1-55542-958-0

Cover art by WILLI BAUM

Manufactured in the United States of America

Office of Educational
Research and Improvement
U.S. Department of Education

Ordering Information

The paperback sourcebooks listed below are published quarterly and can be ordered either by subscription or single copy.

Subscriptions cost $52.00 per year for institutions, agencies, and libraries. Individuals can subscribe at the special rate of $39.00 per year *if payment is by personal check*. (Note that the full rate of $52.00 applies if payment is by institutional check, even if the subscription is designated for an individual.) Standing orders are accepted.

Single copies are available at $12.95 when payment accompanies order. (California, New Jersey, New York, and Washington, D.C., residents please include appropriate sales tax.) For billed orders, cost per copy is $12.95 plus postage and handling.

Substantial discounts are offered to organizations and individuals wishing to purchase bulk quantities of Jossey-Bass sourcebooks. Please inquire.

Please note that these prices are for the academic year 1986–1987 and are subject to change without notice. Also, some titles may be out of print and therefore not available for sale.

To ensure correct and prompt delivery, all orders must give either the *name of an individual* or an *official purchase order number*. Please submit your order as follows:

Subscriptions: specify series and year subscription is to begin.
Single Copies: specify sourcebook code (such as, CC1) and first two words of title.

Mail orders for United States and Possessions, Australia, New Zealand, Canada, Latin America, and Japan to:
Jossey-Bass Inc., Publishers
433 California Street
San Francisco, California 94104

Mail orders for all other parts of the world to:
Jossey-Bass Limited
28 Banner Street
London EC1Y 8QE

New Directions for Community Colleges Series
Arthur M. Cohen, *Editor-in-Chief*
Florence B. Brawer, *Associate Editor*

Contents

Editor's Notes

Since the publication of *Community College Reading Programs* (Ahrendt, 1975), the fabric of reading and developmental education programs in the community college has changed dramatically. Developmental education has become the umbrella under which community colleges, colleges, and universities have placed a wide variety of courses, seminars, and workshops—credit or noncredit—designed to assist "students' development of entry skills in reading, writing, math, speaking, listening, note taking, and studying" (Gruenberg, 1983, p. 2).

Roueche and Snow (1977) developed a working model for developmental education programs in community colleges. Their review of remedial programs was designed to determine the characteristics that successful remedial programs possessed and the factors that contributed to their success. Roueche and Snow focused on programmatic context, philosophy, and rationale. Their work helped to dispel myths about remedial programs, and it defined parameters for a model of successful developmental education program. Maxwell's (1979) landmark work explored the psychological characteristics of the underprepared student. Her extensive review of research and evaluation of developmental education programs provides professionals with a guide for the important task of selection, evaluation, and program review.

Conferences, workshops and in-service meetings—both local and national—have focused on the developmental education student. Numerous articles concerning admission, retention, and the structure and evaluation of developmental education programs have been published. A common set of learner characteristics—lack of confidence, fear of failure, unrealistic goals, poor self-concept, limited academic motivation, learned helplessness, emotional and psychological problems, and learning disabilities—has emerged from reviews of these resources. Using these data as a foundation on which to build, the authors of the chapters in this sourcebook have covered a wide range of topics of concern to developmental education professionals, content area instructors, and administrators. The intent of these contributions is not to be prescriptive but rather seminal.

The various topics discussed by the authors of the chapters in this sourcebook should provide the professional in developmental education with an understanding of the developmental education student's needs and thereby help to structure a learning environment with the whole fabric of the educational process.

The content areas of mathematics and science were chosen simply because these are the two content area courses that all college students

1

experience. Chapters Seven and Eight deal with the mental blocks that many students bring to these subjects—the expectation of failure and the dislike. These chapters attempt to help both the developmental education professional and the content area instructor to deal with student attitudes and build positive concepts toward both mathematics and science.

Student selection, diagnosis, and retention as well as academic support services that are essential to developmental education programs are discussed in Chapters Three and Four of this sourcebook. These chapters provide clear and readily usable resources for the teacher, the administrator, and board members.

One topic long overlooked in the literature on developmental education students—the learning-disabled student—is addressed by Chapter Five. The authors of Chapter Five have condensed a vast amount of research literature and resources for the professional into a chapter that is free from jargon and that affords numerous insights that should be useful to teachers and administrators.

The need still remains for the community college to provide a quality education for all students and to adjust to the educational needs of the students it serves. It does no good to insist that the students adjust to the school. Students cannot escape from the effects of past choices. Thus, both they and the teacher must build on the accumulated past rather than on what might have been if different choices had been made.

If the open-door policy of the community college is to be meaningful, then professionals in developmental education as well as instructors and administrators must become working partners integrated into the total fabric of the educational process. Otherwise, the open door becomes a revolving door.

Kenneth M. Ahrendt
Editor

References

Ahrendt, K. M. *Community College Reading Programs*. Newark, Del.: International Reading Association, 1975. (ED 101 283)

Gruenberg, D. "College Basic Skills Programs: A National Survey." *Journal of Developmental and Remedial Education*, 1983, 6 (3), 2–4, 30–31.

Maxwell, M. *Improving Student Learning Skills: A Comprehensive Guide to Successful Practices and Programs for Increasing the Performance of Underprepared Students*. San Francisco: Jossey-Bass, 1979.

Roueche, J. E., and Snow, J. J. *Overcoming Learning Problems: A Guide to Developmental Education in College*. San Francisco: Jossey-Bass, 1977.

Kenneth M. Ahrendt is associate professor of education at Oregon State University, Corvallis, Oregon.

Thorough integration of developmental education throughout the curriculum is both a practical response to declines in student literacy and an essential step in the protection of the community college's collegiate identity.

Responding to Criticism of Developmental Education

Arthur M. Cohen

Overall declines in student literacy have brought developmental education to the fore in community colleges. Educators who came into the profession fifteen or more years ago had the luxury of dealing with students who had been taught to read and write in the elementary and secondary school systems. Sometime around the mid 1960s, the literacy rates of high school graduates began to decline. The schools were not entirely at fault. As a society we decided that teaching students to drive a car was more important than teaching them how to write. But regardless of the underlying reasons, the community colleges have borne the brunt of that decision. The large proportion of community college students who matriculate with inadequate basic skills preparation dictates that developmental studies will be at the heart of the curriculum and involve all college personnel.

Studies conducted during the past several years by the Center for the Study of Community Colleges testify to this. For example, a curriculum survey conducted in 1977 (Cohen and Brawer, 1982) revealed that one out of every three mathematics courses was being taught at a level less than algebra—that is, arithmetic. The same survey found that three out of eight English classes were admittedly remedial or developmental. More recently, unpublished data on curricula in six large, urban community college districts reveal that 60 percent of the mathematics enrollments

K. M. Ahrendt (ed.). *Teaching the Developmental Education Student.*
New Directions for Community Colleges, no. 57. San Francisco: Jossey-Bass, Spring 1987.

were at the prealgebra level. Further, many students in these districts did not complete courses. Only half of the mathematics students persisted to earn a passing grade, and only 60 percent of the students in English classes successfully completed their courses.

Criticism of large-scale community college efforts in developmental education continues to be raised. Some of the criticisms are valid. Others are not. Some are answerable, while others defy a response. The next six sections summarize some of the objections most often heard.

Criticism One: The Community College Is the Wrong Place to Do Developmental Education

Some people believe that two-year colleges, as institutions of higher learning, should not offer developmental education courses at all. Those who take this position maintain that developmental education properly belongs in the adult schools, in the private sector, or in corporate, on-the-job training programs. This argument is often advanced by college faculty members who feel that their work environment would be improved if students were more able. In response to the question, What would it take to make yours a better course? more than half of the respondents to a 1977 national survey of two-year college science instructors noted, "students better prepared to handle course requirements" (Brawer and Friedlander, 1979, p. 32). That choice far outranked all others on a list of sixteen.

Nevertheless, the argument that the community college is the wrong place to do developmental education simply defies the reality of today's situation. Community college personnel are frankly stuck with the job. There is a tendency for state higher education policy makers to concentrate the remedial function within two-year colleges and to free the state universities and colleges from this responsibility as much as possible (University of Nevada System, 1984; California Postsecondary Education Commission, 1983).

Furthermore, developmental education programs are the logical outgrowth of the focus on access that has characterized the history of American higher education. In the early part of the nineteenth century, higher education was opened to women by a few pioneering women's colleges. Coeducation gradually followed, and it became immoral to bar women from collegiate studies. In the later part of the century, the land-grant colleges opened, making it possible for the children of the less affluent to attend college. It subsequently became immoral to bar people of modest income. In the twentieth century, the civil rights movement of the 1950s and 1960s led to the belief that it was immoral to bar members of ethnic minorities from college. More recently, the various financial aid programs have made it immoral to ban the indigent. Finally, the open-door community college now finds it unfeasible and indeed immoral to bar the ignorant.

Community college involvement in developmental education rests to a large degree on the fact that it is now deemed unacceptable to deny access to college because of inadequate reading, writing, and computation skills.

Criticism Two: Developmental Education Costs Too Much

How many times should the public have to pay to teach the same person how to read? This question is often asked by taxpayers who object to public subsidies for the same type of basic skills instruction at various levels of the educational pipeline. Such objections are often raised as a consequence of the relatively high per-student costs of remedial education. No form of education is easier, and hence cheaper, than a course for literate, self-directed learners. At the same time, no instructional program, not even education in the higher technologies, is more expensive than the instructional media and person-to-person monitoring demanded by slower learners. When it comes to developmental education, questions of impact on faculty and institutional image pale before the issue of cost.

In response to this issue, many community college leaders have replied that it costs less to teach developmental education in two-year colleges than it does in universities and four-year institutions. However, this response is self-defeating in that it projects a negative image and perpetuates the notion of the two-year college as a second-rate institution. Administrators would do better to focus instead on methods of effecting cost savings in the developmental programs themselves. One of the best ways of cutting costs is to use paraprofessional aides—including senior citizens, other lay people, and advanced students. Such aides often find intrinsic rewards in tutoring and are willing to work for a relatively low wage. Furthermore, use of such aides allows the professional instructor to make better use of his or her time. Capps (1984) points out that, in a learning laboratory situation, instructors with adequate tutorial and clerical support are free to spend a relatively large proportion of their time diagnosing learning problems and prescribing appropriate instructional remedies. It simply is not necessary to hire a $30,000-a-year professional faculty member to sit down and work on a one-to-one basis with students.

Criticism Three: Developmental Education Should Be the Responsibility of a Separate Instructional Division, Not the Responsibility of Instructors in the Collegiate Curricula

Many community college practitioners argue that remedial instruction is best administered within a separate department of remedial studies. Students should be tested at entrance, they argue, and those needing basic skills instruction should be required to pass developmental education courses before being allowed to enroll in college-level classes. Separate departments of developmental education, it is further maintained, would put a stop to the unconscionable practice of allowing unprepared students to exercise their so-called right to fail in the collegiate curriculum. In addition, a separate operational division with its own faculty and staff would allow the college to build a cadre of instructors who were experts in remedial instruction. These are compelling arguments, and many policy makers (University of Nevada System, 1984) are convinced that the department model will enhance remedial instruction.

However, there is much to be said for the alternative, namely, the integration of remediation and literacy development throughout the curriculum. First, it is not clear that a separate, one-shot approach to literacy development will be of lasting value to students if literacy skills are not subsequently practiced throughout the curriculum. Richardson, Fisk, and Okun (1983) provide ample evidence that literacy among community college students is on the decline precisely because writing and reading assignments are kept to a minimum. If community colleges are to graduate literate students, then all departments and faculty must take responsibility for basic skills. Second, community colleges run the risk of debilitating the liberal arts curriculum if students without requisite skills are shunted into separate developmental programs. These underprepared students make up a sizable percentage of the student body. If they are not allowed into liberal arts classes, whom will the liberal arts faculty teach? Finally, there is the ethical question of tracking. The open-door philosophy of the two-year college implies that access should not be denied, especially access to the higher learning implied in the word *college*. This does not mean that a student should be allowed to enroll in any class regardless of his or her academic skills. It does mean, however, that developmental studies should not be totally segregated from content area instruction.

These considerations point to the need for every program and every department to have its own developmental education component. This component can take the form of separate developmental courses or, better yet, it can incorporate basic skills instruction into every class. Efforts to integrate basic skills development throughout the curriculum are under way at many community colleges. For example, Sacramento City College (California) offers team-taught courses that combine content material in sociology or psychology with instruction in speech, reading, and writing. The courses are designed to assist students with low reading ability and long histories of academic failure (Bohr, Bray, and Ramirez, 1983; Luvaas-Briggs, 1984). Another example of combined content and basic skills instruction is provided by the Two-Year College Development Center of the State University of New York (State University of New York, 1984). The Center coordinated a statewide faculty development program that was designed to familiarize vocational instructors in the New York community college with strategies that could be used to develop and reinforce basic skills in the classroom.

Criticism Four: There Is Insufficient Articulation
with Secondary Schools

The criticism that there is insufficient articulation with secondary schools is justified. In many states, the early junior colleges grew out of the secondary school districts, and many instructors taught in the high school during the daytime and in the junior college at night. In fact, most of the full-time instructors at early junior colleges were former secondary school teachers who considered themselves colleagues of the teachers at local high schools. Today, however, the professional connections between high schools and community colleges are considerably weakened. Over the past three decades, community college leaders have increasingly identified themselves and their institutions with higher education. In faculty surveys conducted by the Center for the Study of Community Colleges in the 1970s (Cohen and Brawer, 1977), instructors were asked, Have you ever gone into a secondary school to discuss your courses with your counterparts or to recruit students to your program? Only one in ten said that he or she had. The community colleges seemed to be sending a message to the secondary school and its students that they did not care what went on there; they would take students as they came and not worry about course articulation.

However, educational leaders in some states are trying to rebuild the links between higher education and the secondary schools. For example, the academic senate of the University of California, the California state colleges and universities, and the California community colleges recently issued a joint statement on the desired high school academic preparation of matriculating students (Academic Senate for California Community Colleges, 1982). The statement, which was addressed to students, parents, high school teachers, counselors, and administrators, established requisite competencies in reading, writing, and arithmetic, algebra, geometry, and advanced mathematics. Another example stems from Miami–Dade Community College in Florida. The college has collected data on developmental students and presented these data to the secondary schools in its service district. The president of the college has also arranged joint meetings between the community college board of trustees and the board of education to discuss issues of articulation between high schools and the college. Such measures may go a long way in improving the skills of students before they get to the college and thus in resolving the student literacy crisis.

Criticism Five: Faculty Members Do Not Know How
to Teach Literacy

Mention has already been made of the fact that many faculty members are reluctant to shoulder the responsibility for basic skills development. Few instructors enjoy teaching students who do not know how to read and write. Most want bright, capable, literate individuals who are eager to learn the most specialized subject matter that the instructors can put forth. Furthermore, some instructors are little concerned with classroom approaches to literacy development. Faced with increasingly large proportions of ill-prepared students, faculty members often minimize reading and writing requirements, thus contributing to the literacy problem (Richardson, Fisk, and Okun, 1983).

This suggests that the developmental educator should take on the role of staff development specialist. Developmental educators should treat their colleagues in the collegiate curricula as students who need to know more about literacy and the ways in which it can be facilitated. Faculty need to understand that students will only become literate by reading or writing, whether voluntarily, by coercion, or both. Most of the literacy problems faced by community college educators can be traced to declining demands in the classroom, and instructors in the developmental program need to take the lead in turning this situation around.

Besides encouraging instructors to use class assignments that develop literacy skills, developmental education specialists should make content area faculty aware of the learning support services that are available to students. Too often, students do not make use of counseling services, tutorials, learning laboratories, library services, and other types of out-of-class learning support mechanisms provided on campus (Friedlander, 1981). This is due largely to the fact that classroom instructors often have little affiliation with the persons who administer academic support services. The learning laboratory is managed by a learning resource director, the tutorial center is managed by yet another person, and there is consequently very little association between course content and these ancillary support services. Developmental educators should take it upon themselves to bring support services and instructors together.

Criticism Six: Placement and Diagnostic Tests Are Not Valid

Numerous documents added to the ERIC collection during the past three years point to an increased use of testing as a means of assessing the skill levels of entering students and of assigning matriculants with deficiencies to appropriate remedial services. See, for example, the citations on testing in Chapter Nine of this sourcebook. At the same time, many view the tests used by colleges as culturally biased instruments that are not relevant to any content areas except English and mathematics. These objections can and should be countered. Every test, no matter what it tests, is culturally biased. In fact, the entire school system is culturally biased. A culture-free test for admission to certain classes in school would be biased if it did not test students' ability to succeed in those classes. In short, classes are culturally biased. Therefore, a culture-free test would not be valid.

These objections aside, testing can be (and has been) used as an important tool in student literacy development. Miami–Dade Community College (Florida) has a procedure whereby any student who enrolls in more than three classes (either at once or in sequence) or who enrolls in an English or mathematics course is sent to the college testing center to take a placement examination in English and mathematics (McCabe, 1984). On the basis of test results, the student is counseled into different sections of those classes. Of course, this type of student flagging requires a sophisticated student monitoring system, and few institutions have established such a system. In most colleges, students can take course after course without ever having been tested. Testing procedures come into effect only when the student signs up for an English or mathematics class. Even then, the test used may be a crude, homemade instrument devised by members of the department. Nonetheless, more testing is better than less. It is better to find out about student skills deficiencies before a student begins his or her classwork than it is to discover halfway through the term than the student does not have the skills he or she needs to succeed.

Conclusion: What Is at Stake for the Community College?

Integration of developmental education throughout the curriculum is both a practical response to declines in student literacy and an essential step in the protection of the community college's collegiate identity. It is simply not feasible to bar students from collegiate courses until they demonstrate higher levels of reading ability; too few students can read at the levels we would like. But, support services can be mandated, and tutorials and learning laboratory activities can be integrated with classroom instruction. Every instructor can demand reading and writing assignments from students. Entry and exit tests can also be offered to document basic skills gains as students progress through the curriculum.

Such steps will help community college students and, at the same time, assure the integrity of the institution. It is difficult to defend the transfer function when less than 10 percent of student enrollment is accounted for by courses with prerequisites. Yet, it is precisely this enrollment pattern—and concomitant curricular erosion—that is the end result of separate developmental studies departments that segregate ill-prepared students from the collegiate curriculum. For many community college students, particularly minorities and the economically disadvantaged, community colleges represent the only opportunity for access to higher education. It would be a great disservice to these students if the community college failed to attend to the problem of literacy and subsequently lost its legitimacy as a collegiate institution.

References

Academic Senate for California Community Colleges. *Statements on Preparation in English and Mathematics: Competencies Expected of Entering Freshmen and Remedial and Baccalaureate-Level Course Work.* Sacramento: Academic Senate for California Community Colleges, 1982. 112 pp. (ED 222 235)

Bohr, D. H., Bray, D., and Ramirez, K. *Project HELP: Instruction for High Risk, Nontraditional Students.* Sacramento, Calif.: Sacramento City College, 1983. 19 pp. (ED 258 615)

Brawer, F. B., and Friedlander, J. *Science and Social Science in the Two-Year College.* Topical Paper No. 69. Los Angeles: ERIC Clearinghouse for Junior Colleges, 1979. 37 pp. (ED 172 854)

California Postsecondary Education Commission. *Promises to Keep: Remedial Education in California's Public Colleges and Universities.* Sacramento: California Postsecondary Education Commission, 1983. 161 pp. (ED 230 087)

Capps, J. P. *Mathematics Laboratory Focus, Fall 1985.* Somerville, N.J.: Somerset County College, 1984. 16 pp. (ED 255 263)

Cohen, A. M., and Brawer, F. B. *The Two-Year College Instructor Today.* New York: Praeger, 1977.

Cohen, A. M., and Brawer, F. B. *The American Community College.* San Francisco: Jossey-Bass, 1982.

Friedlander, J. *Why Don't Poorly Prepared Students Seek Help?* Los Angeles: Center for the Study of Community Colleges, 1981. 14 pp. (ED 203 901)

Luvaas-Briggs, L. "Integrating Basic Skills with College Content Instruction." *Journal of Developmental and Remedial Education,* 1984, 7 (2), 6-9, 31.

McCabe, R. H. *A Status Report on the Comprehensive Educational Reform at Miami–Dade Community College.* Miami, Fla.: Miami–Dade Community College, 1984. 10 pp. (ED 238 481)

Richardson, R. C., Jr., Fisk, E. C., and Okun, M. A. *Literacy in the Open-Access College.* San Francisco: Jossey-Bass, 1983.

State University of New York. *Basic Skills in Postsecondary Occupational Education: Faculty Development Resource Manual. Materials Developed and Used by New York State Two-Year College Staff in the Role of Faculty Trainers.* Albany: Two-Year College Development Center, State University of New York, 1984. 101 pp. (ED 253 269)

University of Nevada System. *An Assessment of Developmental and Remedial Education in the University of Nevada System.* Reno: University of Nevada System, 1984. 31 pp. (ED 258 621)

Arthur M. Cohen is director of the ERIC Clearinghouse for Junior Colleges and a professor of higher education at the University of California, Los Angeles.

*The politics of remediation reflects the struggle by
community colleges to develop a distinctive identity.*

The Politics of Remediation

Dennis McGrath, Martin B. Spear

The politics of remediation over the past twenty years expresses the struggle by legislators, state agencies, educators, and other groups to define the
role and nature of the community college. The discourse of remediation,
and the policy debates that surround it, are primary ways that we argue
about what community colleges are as institutions. In these debates, community colleges have been variously understood as extensions of high
school, as community centers, as somewhat unusual versions of traditional
colleges, and as a distinctively new educational experiment.

Remediation and the Struggle for Identity

During the 1960s, the rapid growth of community colleges produced an attempt on their part to project a distinctive identity by defining
their transfer, remedial, vocational, and community roles. This initial
effort also spawned a first generation of criticism, which largely reproduced the "great school debates" of earlier decades concerning public education. These were played out as contrasting conceptions of the social and
educational mission of the community college, leading to differing standards of evaluation and divergent conclusions about community colleges'
role and effectiveness. The discussion of remediation and of institutional
responsibility for underprepared students served as a symbolic politics, in
which arguments about very specific issues were tied to much larger

K. M. Ahrendt (ed.). *Teaching the Developmental Education Student.*
New Directions for Community Colleges, no. 57. San Francisco: Jossey-Bass, Spring 1987.

debates about the role of schooling in influencing poverty and the class structure.

The remedial function of the community college first became articulated in the 1960s, with the massive expansion of higher education. The construction of hundreds of new community colleges, the formal open-admissions policy of the City University of New York, and the expansion of massive state higher education systems in California and New York promoted a tremendous influx of new students who would otherwise never have been able to attend college. This large group of first-generation college students placed great strain on the traditional curriculum and pedagogy of colleges, challenging the institutions that received these students to redefine their missions and rethink their curricular structures and pedagogical practices. This challenge was most acute for community colleges attempting to establish their roles and identities within higher education primarily through the articulation of their "remedial function."

In the early 1960s, the primary categories available in conventional educational thought for understanding the problems of learners judged to be not yet qualified to engage in college-level work were the conceptions of remedial and compensatory education. The notion of compensatory education was introduced into educational discourse following World War II and gained substantial legitimacy with the Elementary and Secondary Education Act of 1965. Compensatory education was understood as "those efforts designed to make up for the debilitating consequences of discrimination and poverty" (Chazen, 1973, p. 35). Such programs were seen as efforts to offset the cultural deprivation experienced by students in home environments that did not provide support for education.

While the language of compensatory education remained dominant in public education throughout the 1960s and influenced such programs as Head Start, Get Set, and many other efforts, the notion of remediation primarily guided program construction in the community college. The concept of remediation can be seen as initially more attractive to community college administrators and faculty than compensatory education was: By concentrating on specific academic skills, it supported an educational/social mission compatible with the traditional college model. In other words, community colleges could be understood as engaged in traditional academic instruction, with the only difference being that they admitted large numbers of students who required intensive work on specific skills before entering the regular curriculum. Remediation encouraged talk of "skills" and "skill deficiencies," understood in relatively discrete and mechanical ways, and suggested that the solution lay in the development of an appropriate educational technology. Understood metaphorically, remediation employs a medical model, in which specific weaknesses are diagnosed, appropriate treatments are prescribed, and the learner/patient is evaluated to determine the effects of treatment (Clowes, 1982–1983, p. 4).

Compensatory education was much more threatening, since programs designed to combat cultural deprivation of students seemed likely to redefine the college more as a social or community action agency than as an educational institution. The establishment of remedial courses and programs thus permitted community college educators to distinguish themselves and their mission from that of the public schools and to ally with four-year institutions, many of which also were making tentative efforts at remediation.

By the early 1970s, commentators had established several well-developed lines of criticism, focusing both on the function of community colleges and on their effectiveness. One line of criticism centered on the role of community colleges within the larger political economy and on their function in reproducing the class structure. This view held that attempts by community college leaders to emphasize the academic dimension of their institutions and differentiate them from high schools were largely unsuccessful and failed to recognize the role that two-year colleges play in helping to isolate traditional colleges and universities from the growing numbers of nontraditional students. Jencks and Riesman (1968) first articulated this concern by arguing that the new community colleges "are a safety valve releasing pressures that might otherwise disrupt the dominant system. They contain these pressures and allow the universities to go their own way without facing the full consequences of excluding the dull-witted or uninterested majority. . . . We doubt that the community college movement will lead to significant innovations in academic theory or practice" (pp. 491–492). Later critics analyzed this "safety valve" function carefully, arguing that both the structure and the culture of the community college were excessively vocational. This, they held, limited working-class students, serving to reproduce their class position by "cooling out" their expectations and channeling them into low-status positions and away from the university-parallel programs that could prepare them for further academic work and professional careers.

Karabel (1972), for instance, asserted that the community college is a key element within the American system of class-based education, in which lower-class students are tracked into occupational programs as a way of deflecting their aspirations for higher degrees and higher-status employment. Zwerling (1976) complemented this analysis by arguing that community colleges "have become just one more barrier put between the poor and the disenfranchised and a decent and respectable stake in the social system which they seek" (p. xvii). Their function, in his view, is to "assist in channeling young people to essentially the same relative position[s] in the social structure that their parents occupy" (p. 33). Zwerling, like Karabel, focused on the heavily vocational emphasis of community colleges as compared to four-year institutions and argued that the powerful vocational thrust of the curriculum and the career counseling of students both serve to control mobility between classes by tracking students into lower-level technical and paraprofessional jobs. Thus, the expansion of occupational education was "an ingenious way of providing large numbers of students with access to schooling without disturbing the shape of the social structure" (p. 61). Community colleges, with their primary emphases on remediation and on development of low-level technical skills, were seen as taking on the worst characteristics of the industrial plant and the junior high school. The expansion of remedial programs throughout the 1960s and 1970s could be seen as an extension of tracking, which further defined the community college as a noncollegiate institution that insulated four-year colleges and universities from nontraditional students.

This powerful style of criticism raised disturbing questions about the nature of the new community college, but it had little impact on actual curricular structures and pedagogical practices. In part, this effect was due to the hostility these critics engendered among community college educators. Also, aside from Zwerling's sketch of what a class-sensitive pedagogy would look like, it was difficult to see how to bring these analyses to bear on the administrative structures and classroom practices of the schools.

Besides the political-economy criticism, a second line developed, which focused on the ways in which curriculum and pedagogy would have to be reconstructed to meet the needs of nontraditional students. This analysis, which we term the educational effectiveness criticism, held that traditional college curricula and pedagogy could not deal effectively with the new students now entering higher education and so had to be reconceived. But, unlike Jencks and Riesman, the educational effectiveness critics held that the community colleges, and not the elite schools, would provide the leadership in developing a new educational theory and practice that would be effective with nontraditional students. Advocates of this approach believed that they could develop ways to reconstruct the curricular structures, student services, and pedagogy of community colleges to make them inviting and supportive environments for nontraditional students.

While recognizing the consequences that higher education had for class structure, the educational effectiveness critics softened this issue in several ways. They argued that nontraditional students should not be identified with minorities or with the lower class and, countering the political economy view, held that it is illegitimate for public policy to shift the meaning of educational equality from individual to group mobility. Cohen and Brawer (1982) were most explicit in articulating the liberal challenge to the socialist goals of the political economy critics, arguing that no form of schooling can "break down class distinctions . . . or move entire ethnic groups from one social stratum to another" (p. 353). Cross (1971) was particularly forceful in defining "new students." She described these students as new to higher education because only in an age of open admissions would they be considered "college material"; they ranked in the lowest third of high school graduates on traditional tests of academic achievement.

Cross's conception contradicts identification of nontraditional or underprepared students with racial minorities. She argued that most are drawn from the white working class, but many come from the middle class as well. Later (1976), she argued that "two-thirds are first-generation college students . . . over one-half are white, about 25 percent are black, and about 15 percent other minorities. . . . The majority of high school graduates ranking in the lowest academic third are white" (p. 6).

As educational effectiveness critics examined the response of colleges to these new students, however, they found that programs and pedagogy remained extremely traditional and largely ineffective. Cross (1976), for instance, argued that remediation efforts have helped mostly those on the borderline of acceptable academic performance, but that "we have not found any magic key to equality of educational opportunity through remediation" (p. 9). Further, remediation efforts operated only on the fringes of higher education and had not penetrated into the instructional core of colleges.

Roueche (1968), from his first national study of remedial programs, echoed Cross's criticism that institutional remediation efforts tended to be limited, marginal, and largely ineffective. In his review of programs in the late 1960s, Roueche argued that "as many as 90 percent of all students assigned or advised into remedial programs never completed them . . . little wonder that critics of community colleges soon referred to the open-door policy as a 'revolving door policy'" (p. 48). Most of the remedial programs that he surveyed consisted mainly of watered-down versions of regular college-level courses, preparatory in nature and taught by regular academic departments. Because of this rather grim picture, Roueche, like Cross, applauded the more comprehensive programs that were developed in the 1970s, which included a broad range of educational services and teaching strategies and had separately organized divisions of remedial education with all-volunteer teaching and counseling staffs (Roueche and Kirk, 1973). These programs pioneered the "instructional revolution" judged necessary for colleges to be educationally effective.

For the major advocates of this position, such as Cross, Roueche, and Cohen, the instructional revolution should be based on the principles of mastery learning, the individualization of instruction, and the introduction of new learning technologies. While these are first introduced into remedial programs as efforts to improve the instruction of low-skill students, this approach to pedagogy should be spread through the entire curriculum, both in community colleges and in higher education generally. In this way, concentration on remediation, according to the educational effectiveness critics, can give the community college a distinctive identity as the vanguard institution producing the pedagogical and programmatic innovations that will ultimately be adopted throughout higher education.

The emergence of developmental programs in the 1970s muted the impact of the educational effectiveness criticisms and completed the movement away from more traditional, heavily cognitive understandings of remediation. Partly as a response to the perceived failure to successfully move large numbers of underprepared students into the general curriculum, and partly as a humanistic reaction to the widespread development of educational "technology," developmental educators argued that bringing students "up to college level" in their "basic skills" (the concern that had dominated earlier conceptions of remediation) was only a part, and maybe not the most important part, of what the community college ought to be doing for the students who were overflowing the remedial classrooms. Drawing on a rich set of educational, psychological, political, and even ethical traditions, they said that even though few students ever successfully made the transition from the special precollege programs into the traditional curriculum, those programs were not failures because of that. Instead, developmental programs were to be understood as encouraging and facilitating the full mental, moral, and emotional growth of students, whose lives might be enriched by their coming to know, appreciate, and ultimately express their full selves as members of society and as members of their particular social and racial minorities. Developmental practices and strategies conceived with the objectives of developing personal consciousness, changing affective styles, encouraging social competence, and enriching the lives of students, their families, and their communities—despite the fact that such things are bound to be notoriously hard to evaluate—became progressively merged with the more traditional practices of remediation. This merger, which occurred within many programs during the 1970s and 1980s, is astonishing in many ways, since each program draws on very different sources for its sense of mission, underlying epistemology, vocabulary, and practices. Indeed, each often has explicitly defined itself against the others and has sought to characterize itself as trying to accomplish different ends by different means and for different reasons.

Looking back from our current perspective, we can see that the lines of criticism developed by both political economy and educational effectiveness advocates were important, but neither was fully successful at articulating an approach that would adequately define the identity of the community college and its mission with nontraditional students. The pedagogical revolution hoped for by the educational effectiveness proponents has not occurred; indeed, it has largely been preempted by the emergence of the notion of developmental education, while ever larger numbers of students now enter our vocational and remedial programs. Working-class and minority students are even more concentrated in community colleges, while transfer rates to four-year institutions have declined precipitously. The expansion of higher education during the past twenty-five years has reproduced the traditional two-tiered structure of education—one for the elite and another for the masses—that has long existed at the primary and secondary levels (Bastian and others, 1985). The infusion of nontraditional students, especially those from racial minorities and from the white working and lower classes, has provided some additional opportunities while still preserving the dual educational structure.

The Quest for a Vision

It is not our intention here to be unduly critical of remedial and developmental programs, since, in the absence of the community-based literacy programs advocated by Kozol (1985), they represent the major societal response to adult illiteracy. However, we do want to argue that remedial/developmental understandings of education have become diffused through the community college to the point where those understandings have come to constitute the academic environment, and that in remedial programs language use is fundamentally trivialized as being either a matter of skills acquisition or personal expression, so that the "remedialization" of community colleges contributes to the perpetuation of the dual structure of American education.

The broad processes by which even the university-parallel programs have become remedialized are clear enough, although the particulars of the story differ from state to state and even from college to college. Counseling and advising practices that place high value on maximization of student choice and opportunity; admission and registration policies that frequently render testing and placement problematic; funding and financial aid policies that encourage rapid movement into regular college courses or concurrent placement in them; the general cultural disarticulation of even the best-prepared nontraditional students from traditional academic classrooms—all these phenomena have resulted in a blurring of the distinction between the remedial/developmental function and the traditional academic function. Put crudely, the appearance of large numbers of underprepared students in the classrooms of traditional academic disciplines has led traditional academics more and more frequently to mimic the practices and vocabulary of remedial/developmental programs, which suggest either a mechanical "skills" orientation or a social service mission aimed at individual affective development.

What is most astonishing about remedial/developmental programs is the way that language use is implicitly devalued in them. To understand this, remember how language enters into the academic program and into the lives of more traditional students at more traditional sorts of schools. For them, reading and writing (and, analogously, mathematics) are not matters of mastering semantic, syntactic, and orthographic correctness, as in remedial programs, nor are they matters of students being provided with opportunities for intellectual, esthetic, and moral growth—"finding one's own voice," as in the developmental variants. For traditional students, the deploying of the competencies that programs try to remediate is part of a style of life that is rich and meaningful beyond the classroom. In other words, academic education is for them a system of progressive initiation into various communities of discourse. Not so for remedial or developmental students; in these programs, language appears as rules to be mastered, rules divorced from any meaningful adult use of language. Semesters and possibly years of drudgery will precede any useful and significant outcomes for remedial students. If traditional students had to engage in countless essentially pointless exercises before any real engagement with academics could begin, probably far fewer bachelor's degrees would be awarded. The developmental solution to the debilitating apathy associated with dictionary exercises and mechanical drills is to put a much greater emphasis on personal expression as the genre that will carry the developing language skills. Thus, little reaction papers, opinion papers, journals, personal narratives, and the like are thought to be intrinsically rewarding as well as educationally worthwhile and so have largely displaced drills and exercises as the primary modes of activity in the remedial/developmental classroom. But what theory of human behavior suggests that students would be willing to spend a significant portion of their adult lives engaged in expressive activity that lacks the seriousness signalled by powerful communal supports and constraints?

Recent studies document the intensification of the two-tiered structure of American education. Today it no longer has the explicit form of one system for whites and one for blacks. Instead, what we see is erosion of the standards of literacy and inquiry throughout much of education, with only pockets of rigor and high quality left for those able to pay the tuition at more elite institutions. Virtually all the studies of classroom experience at the secondary and college levels document a "leveling down" of the standards of what counts as sophisticated language use and rigorous inquiry. At the secondary level, one research team finds class content increasingly simplified and reduced to lists to be memorized, while in-class assignments replace homework (Sedlak, Wheeler, Pullin, and Cusick, 1985). Another study of high schools characterizes the process as the formulation of "private treaties" between students and teachers to limit the amount and quality of coursework (Powell, Cohen, and Farrar, 1985). At the community college level, this analysis is complemented by the work of Richardson and his colleagues. Their study of a community college system argues that the traditional role of written language in the curriculum has been undermined and replaced by more fragmented and limited language use. In their terms, this is the shift from "texting," understood as the use of reading and writing to comprehend or compose connected language, to "bitting," the production or understanding of fragmented language when the student is presented with specific external cues (Richardson, Fisk, and

Okun, 1983). As in the high school studies, this erosion of literacy is produced through a series of "bargains" or "negotiations" at the classroom level: Teachers, committed to one particular instructional style, the classroom lecture, and to the limited instructional goal of "information transfer," respond to underprepared and indifferent students by simply watering down the requirements. Faculty both "transfer" less complex information to students via lectures and demand much less literate behavior from students by replacing term papers and essays with multiple-choice exams. The consequences for the institution are that the norms of literate activity are renegotiated downward, ultimately altering the entire intellectual climate of the school (McGrath and Spear, 1985b).

The debate about remediation provides a useful way to understand the mission that makes the community colleges historically important, what makes them worth having and worth saving, and what involves them in bringing the socially and economically disenfranchised classes into full integration with the dominant culture, full participation in our civic life, and equal opportunity for advancement. If community colleges are to articulate a distinct identity and educational role, then they must find ways to put language use at the center of their curricula and develop pedagogical practices powerful enough to prepare nontraditional students adequately for the literacy requirements of academic and professional careers.

None of the alternative and weaker understandings of the social and political missions of community colleges acknowledges the full dimensions of the literacy problem nor develops pedagogical settings and practices to address it. The liberal understanding suggests practices focusing on individual achievement in a competitive setting, which is conceived as essentially meritocratic. The nontraditionality of students is largely addressed by the development of large social service organizations within the collegiate structure. Vocationalists opt for a pedagogy of training—rote memorization, the mastering of myriad essentially meaningless tasks, and individual definition within a rigid professional hierarchy. The social activist tries to bring the student to full self-consciousness as a member of an oppressed group, both for appreciation of the unique values and achievements of that group and for collective political action to alter existing social and political arrangements. The remedial and developmental educator attempts to reconstruct community colleges and make them adequate settings for nontraditional students, but such attempts lack the educational vision and the pedagogical practices appropriate to countering the leveling-down of literacy standards. Each approach draws on different theoretical traditions, but they are alike in inhibiting the promotion of sophisticated writing and interpretation through the trivialization of language use. It is interesting, and of the first importance, that none of these implied pedagogical styles is directly concerned with the consistent and sustained use of powerful and sophisticated language competencies, and all may be directly countering it by their insistence on the mechanical, informational, and expressive functions of language use.

Our own experience suggests that only a carefully designed, sustained process of faculty and curriculum development that permits the collegiate "renogotiation" of the norms and practices of literacy can have sufficient power to counter the almost overwhelming downward drift of expectations, which has a devastating effect on the academic and occupational destinies of students (McGrath and Spear, 1985a). If nontraditional students are to be adequately prepared for academic success, then there must be substantial transformations in their very conceptions of education and in their sense of themselves as learners. Settings must be constructed to help nontraditional students experience education as something more than simply memorization and recitation. Put another way, they must be initiated into the intellectual community and enticed to participate in its practices. But for students to be prepared for initiation into academic and professional communities, they must engage in and experience the real nature of the intellectual activity. This, we strongly hold, requires a substantial alteration and upgrading of the role of literate activity in the curriculum. This is the reconstruction of the community college needed for it to fulfill its mission in the 1980s.

References

Bastian, A., Fruchter, N., Gittell, M., Greer, C., and Haskins, K. "Choosing Equality: The Case for Democratic Schooling." *Social Policy*, 1985, 34–51.

Chazen, M. (ed.) *Compensatory Education*. London: Butterworth, 1973.

Clowes, D. A. "More Than a Definitional Problem." *Current Issues in Higher Education*, 1982–1983, *1*, 1–12.

Cohen, A. M., and Brawer, F. B. *The American Community College*. San Francisco: Jossey-Bass, 1982.

Cross, K. P. *Beyond the Open Door: New Students to Higher Education*. San Francisco: Jossey-Bass, 1971.

Cross, K. P. *Accent on Learning: Improving Instruction and Reshaping the Curriculum*. San Francisco: Jossey-Bass, 1976.

Jencks, C., and Riesman, D. *The Academic Revolution*. New York: Doubleday, 1968.

Karabel, J. "Community Colleges and Social Stratification: Submerged Class Conflict in American Higher Education." *Harvard Educational Review*, 1972, *42* (4), 521–562.

Kozol, J. *Illiterate America*. New York: Anchor Press, 1985.

McGrath, D., and Spear, M. B. "Renegotiating Literacy Standards: Writing, Pedagogy and Faculty Development." Ford Foundation Urban Community College Transfer Opportunities Program Working Paper, New York: August 1985a.

McGrath, D., and Spear, M. B. "Review of *Literacy in the Open-Access College.*" *Community/Junior College Quarterly of Research and Practice*, 1985b, *9* (4), 382–387.

Powell, A., Cohen, D., and Farrar, E. *The Shopping-Mall High School*. Boston: Houghton Mifflin, 1985.

Richardson, R. C., Jr., Fisk, E. C., and Okun, M. A. *Literacy in the Open-Access College*. San Francisco: Jossey-Bass, 1983.

Roueche, J. E. *Salvage, Redirection, or Custody?* Washington, D.C.: American Association of Junior Colleges, 1968.

Roueche, J. E., and Kirk, R. W. *Catching Up: Remedial Education*. San Francisco: Jossey-Bass, 1973.

Sedlak, M., Wheeler, C., Pullin, D., and Cusick, P. *Classroom Perspectives on High School Reform*. New York: Teachers College Press, 1985.

Zwerling, L. S. *Second Best: The Crisis of the Community College*. New York: McGraw-Hill, 1976.

Dennis McGrath, professor of sociology, and Martin B. Spear, professor of philosophy, are codirectors of the Transfer Opportunities Program at Community College of Philadelphia.

Learning assistance programs are vital to the pedagogical mission of the community college.

Academic Support Services for Developmental and High-Risk Students in Community Colleges

Gilbert J. Carbone

In a report entitled *Assisting Student Learning,* Barshis (1984) described various academic support services provided by community colleges. These services are designed to achieve two objectives: one directly related to students' learning skills, the other involving the skills of the teacher.

Direct support services are designed to enhance students' chances of success. They include assessment and placement activities, remedial course work, learning assistance laboratories, tutoring, counseling, and instruction in the use of educational technology.

The second objective involves attempts to achieve improvements in the instructional process through professional staff development. This objective includes a wide variety of in-service activities, ranging from computer literacy training to team teaching with off-campus practitioners. It can provide opportunities for pedagogical training or incentives for conducting instructional research related to teaching and learning.

According to Barshis (1984, p. 3), the overall goal of such activities is to achieve "individualized instruction within a highly structured learn-

K. M. Ahrendt (ed.). *Teaching the Developmental Education Student.*
New Directions for Community Colleges, no. 57. San Francisco: Jossey-Bass, Spring 1987.

ing program." He cites the observation of Benjamin Bloom that such activity involves dealing with "alterable variables in the teaching/learning process that could bring conventional group instruction closer to the superior levels possible in one-on-one tutoring or individualized instruction" (Barshis, 1984, p. 5).

Learning Assistance Versus Support Services

Before proceeding, it is necessary to agree on some terms. *Academic support services* is probably not the most appropriate term for the activities discussed in this chapter. I prefer the term *learning assistance program*. It refers to various activities designed to advance the arts of learning and teaching. The goals of all such activities are (or should be) the same: development of the student's abilities to acquire and use information and enhancement of the teacher's ability to facilitate that development.

Effective learning assistance requires more than just making remediation services available to underprepared students. Palmer (1984) reviewed a number of studies and concluded that skill improvement did not result either from taking reading or writing courses or from merely making progress toward a degree. At about the same time, Bender and Lukenbill (1984, p. 17) charged that the community colleges diminished their effectiveness by "the absence of systematic and continuous development of the human resources of the institution itself." Both observations have implications for learning assistance programming.

Remediation Plus

This chapter, then, will deal with learning assistance in the broadest sense. At this point, it would be useful to make a distinction between developmental students and high-risk students. We can hope that all students are developmental: Good readers can become better readers. Good writers never quit perfecting their skill. Perhaps the same thing can be said of teachers. Excellent teachers can improve their art. However, not all developmental students are high-risk students. While students in the second group deserve the special focus of learning assistance programs, those programs must not be limited to remediation of chronically skill-deficient students, lest our results fall short of our expectations.

Other writers have added to Barshis's (1984) list of services that are part of the mosaic of a comprehensive learning assistance program. Flamm and others (1984) saw consultation, outreach and recruiting, and precollege programs as desirable features. Friedlander (1982) suggested that early and midterm intervention strategies should be on the list. Cramer and Liberty (1981) commented that a probation policy, coordinated with other services, was an important aspect. Stumhofer (1984) described academic profiles developed by the admissions office on each entering student as a technique to support the learning program.

Keys to Effective Programs

Roueche's (1984) report on a University of Texas study of college and university responses to low-achieving students provides a convenient checklist of the characteristics of successful programs. Noting that no institution could escape the problem of skill-deficient students, Roueche and his associates synthesized eleven "elements of success" from the information provided by institutions that reported 50 percent or better retention rates in developmental programs:

- Strong administrative support
- Mandatory assessment and placement upon entry
- Structured courses and follow-up of nonattenders
- Award of credit for developmental courses
- Flexible completion features
- Multiple learning systems, accessed through learning prescriptions based on assessment data
- Use of only volunteer instructors in developmental courses
- Extensive use of peer tutors
- Frequent monitoring of student behaviors
- Interfacing with subsequent courses
- Program evaluation based on adequate data collection procedures.

Noel, Levitz, and Kaufman (1982, p. 7) also saw that developmental or remedial services alone were insufficient to ensure student success. These writers described a comprehensive program in terms of the outcomes that students should seek: "Students must learn to motivate themselves, to understand their learning strengths and weaknesses, to negotiate the academic and social system, to adapt effective and efficient methods of processing information, and to alter previously established attitudes about their own potential and their sense of self-worth. These needs are best met by college programs that provide a range of services that attend to special developmental needs while considering the adjustment of the whole person to the college environment." These authors added transition and orientation activities and study or survival skills to the list of desirable learning assistance services, noting that such support mechanisms provided a common denominator for components of the program. Not surprisingly, however, these authors commented that responses gathered in their extensive survey of two- and four-year colleges suggested that the personal characteristics and attitudes of campus professionals were of greater importance than the design and structure of the learning assistance program.

Effective Teaching: A Prime Ingredient

Boylan (1985) has emphasized the importance of professional service providers in dealing with developmental and high-risk students. In a document identified as the third revision of a statement on underpreparedness written for the National Association for Developmental Education (NADE), Boylan commented that poor academic performance often stems from poor teaching as well as from deficient student skill development (Boylan, 1985). Noting the national interest in educational excellence that arose in the mid 1980s, the draft NADE statement cautioned that achievement of excellence would require a national investment in the improvement of college teaching skills. Other recommendations in the proposed NADE statement included increased support for research on teaching and learning, increased efforts to disseminate examples of outstanding efforts to strengthen the skills of underprepared students, and recognition that all students can profit from improvements in educational practices and learning assistance services.

A Multicampus Learning Assistance Model

Given adequate resources, it is possible to design a model system of learning assistance services for the typically diverse clientele of the community college and for the practitioners who function there. One such attempt, with which I was associated, occurred in the Washington state system of community colleges. It was a project, supported by a two-year FIPSE grant, designed to stimulate improvements in campus learning assistance programs. The summary of the final project report describes the Learning Assistance Support System (LASS) initiated by that project (Carbone and Torgerson, 1983).

In recognition of a need to improve the delivery of basic skills instruction and other learning assistance experiences to its students, the Washington community college system established a support system designed, first, to encourage resource sharing; second, to promote professional growth; and third, to assess the status of developmental education in the state's twenty-seven two-year colleges. The project sought to promote planning, coordinate efforts, provide technical assistance, encourage research, and increase campus-level support for learning assistance activities.

A major aspect of the project involved identification and cataloging of resource materials that would be useful to developmental educators and program directors in the various colleges. During the course of the project, more than 900 such references were processed. A brief description of these resources was indexed through a system of twenty-eight general topic titles and twenty-eight specific program items. The information was stored in the college system's central computer, and it was available on line through terminals located on the campuses. Extensive resource sharing occurred as a result.

Project activities also included five workshops on technical subjects, two general-interest statewide meetings, production of thirteen videotapes describing exemplary programs and instructional techniques, establishment of a statewide professional organization for developmental educators, and publication of thirty newsletters and other bulletins that described note-worthy aspects of learning assistance programs. Services were extended to public school personnel, vocational schools, Indian and Hispanic education centers, and colleges and universities in Washington and neighboring states.

Project activities tended to increase the visibility of developmental education program strengths and weaknesses. Staff interaction with college administration officers was instrumental in establishing a systemwide committee composed of developmental education program directors. This committee provided a mechanism for improving communications about developmental education programming throughout the decision-making structure both at the campus and at the system levels.

Four task groups cooperated in publication of a document entitled *Platform for Excellence* (Washington State Board for Community College Education, 1983). Designed as a planning tool, the forty-page booklet reviewed the status of developmental education, program organization and management, assessment practices and materials, and instruction in English as a second language. It also presented a series of public policy recommendations related to improving and sustaining developmental education programming in the Washington two-year college system.

Implicit in the philosophy of an open-admissions college is the promise that programs and services will address the needs and skill levels of entering students. The *Platform for Excellence* of the Washington project sought to fulfill that promise by recommending a set of minimum characteristics that a truly comprehensive learning assistance program should have. The list began with the suggestion that the program should be based on a written statement of purpose and program philosophy. Common understanding of the goals of a program with campuswide implications is absolutely necessary.

The second requisite characteristic identified in the booklet was the appointment of a program coordinator with sufficient administrative support to ensure campuswide access and credibility. Other recommendations called for funding at least at the level of other instructional programs, coordination with an assessment and placement program, and an attendance policy that encouraged diligent student participation. Other features of a model program included competency-based, self-paced learning opportunities and use of computer-based instruction.

A further recommendation was that program visibility and staffing with professionals of diverse educational backgrounds were thought to be key to program success. A close association between the learning assistance program and the college's professional development program was considered essential. Finally, it was suggested that a high-quality learning assistance program would include a bridge to a counseling and advising program that provided for "next-step" planning and action activities for students progressing through the system.

A Model Campus-Based Program

The Institute for Developmental Educational Activities (IDEA) operated by Luzerne County Community College in Nanticoke, Pennsylvania, is an excellent example of a campus-based learning assistance program. This well-defined and broadly functioning program has parlayed a combination of institutional and grant funding into a truly comprehensive program. A list of the elements of this program reads like a glossary of possible activities for developmental educators. However, rather than just offering a smorgasbord of elective services, the program required assessment and screening in order to match learners with services in nearly all aspects of the program. Because learning assistance programs must compete with more traditional programs for resources, the notion of proper placement of students within the learning assistance program deserves special emphasis. A record of successful completions, based on hard data, is the best way to ensure continued support, both financial and political.

The menu of IDEA services included a reading clinic, a project for talented and gifted students, and a remedial program for underachievers that not only served the college's adult learners but reached down to the area's elementary and secondary students as well. A basic life skills component offered learning opportunities in developing social and academic skills, including tutoring as required. Other services included diagnostic testing, special seminars, and programs for targeted audiences preparing for GED, SAT, and ACT testing.

In something of a departure from tradition, the IDEA program participated in an assessment of the training needs and training programs of businesses and educational institutions in its service area. Contractual training programs were then provided for interested firms in cooperation with the state's customized job training program. In addition, a training resources directory was published, a conference on business training needs was held, and plans were made to participate in development of a business incubator facility.

Other IDEA services included an academic placement testing component that screened all incoming first-year students, a career planning program, tutorial services, special services for students on academic probation, and regularly scheduled academic skills seminars. Billing itself as the provider of holistic approaches to meeting individual student needs, IDEA was developed around the central goal of carrying out the college's open-admissions philosophy.

Educator, Heal Thyself

It should be of more than passing interest that many writers on the subject of developmental education programs make comments or recommendations about the quality of teaching and the professional development of teachers. It should also be somewhat to the chagrin of our profession that recognition of this significant connection has been slow in coming. Perhaps it is more accurate to say that doing something about improving the quality of teaching has not always been a high priority of budget decision makers or of faculty. Even with much of the electorate and many politicians flushed with fears of a nation at risk, setting higher student achievement standards seems to have been the favored solution. The alternative of providing resources to deal with the causes of underachievement, rather than with the symptoms, received little attention.

Who, then, will lead in the efforts to improve learning skills and teaching performance? The answer is, of course, that we all must accept responsibility for reordering priorities so that the desired results are achieved. The list must include more than the individuals responsible for learning assistance or professional development programs. It should include department heads who evaluate performance, members of tenure review committees, and persons who sit at the table during collective bargaining negotiating sessions. Students must be involved, too. They must be willing to demand that community colleges deliver what they purport to deliver: educational opportunities attuned to students' needs.

Community colleges that enroll significant numbers of skill-deficient students face unique administrative and programming problems. The real significance of this statement lies in whether the institution finds appropriate solutions to those problems. None of the features of the learning assistance programs described in this chapter are particularly unique or revolutionary. Rather, they are practical applications that resulted when leadership met need head on. Opportunities for leadership can and must be created by administrators, legislators, and grant makers. The responsibility for seizing those opportunities belongs to everyone.

Progress takes time and persistence. After nearly eight years of a placement testing program that has grown to cover virtually all incoming students in New Jersey public colleges and universities, a report by the New Jersey State Department of Higher Education (1985) noted that data obtained through the testing program indicated great progress in improving remedial programs. However, the report also indicated that the program should be extended to part-time students, that basic skills students should not be allowed to pass unless they achieved a minimum competency level, and that site visitations and model program dissemination should be increased.

The final recommendation of the New Jersey report recognized the significance of superior teaching in the war on skill deficiency. Unfortunately, the recommendation falls short of the mark. The report urges that information on effective instructional procedures be distributed to secondary schools in the state. This is not surprising in light of an earlier report by Morante and others (1982) that the first five years of the New Jersey program failed to produce evidence of meaningful change in the proficiency levels of entering college students. However, postsecondary institutions cannot expect to staunch the flow of skill-deficient students merely by urging secondary schools to do better. Community colleges in particular must be prepared to serve the adult learner who needs special assistance. To the credit of New Jersey, its Department of Higher Education has plans to initiate a state-level professional development program to augment the efforts of individual colleges and the secondary schools.

Community Colleges Respond

Those familiar with the history of American higher education know of the mid-nineteenth-century beginnings of the elective curriculum. In one sense, the current provisions for learning assistance services are an extension of that movement. Just as the higher educators of the 1800s struggled with the idea of broadening the course of study, present-day educators face the issue of the need to remediate. Community colleges have responded, not only for the students who come directly from the secondary schools but also for those from the ranks of the more than twenty million functionally illiterate adults in our nation.

Community colleges have also responded to those who have asked, How many times must you teach them to read? Our answer is, As many times as it takes for them to become functional readers. The challenge is to have the courage of our convictions, to put learning assistance in a place of prominence on the campus, to work for adequate funding for the programs, and to develop an active commitment to improved teaching.

James A. Garfield, the twentieth president of the United States, has been credited with describing a well-endowed college as a log with a student on one end and Mark Hopkins on the other. This tribute to excellent teaching is not related to the observation by Benjamin Bloom about individualized instruction noted earlier in this chapter. One-on-one is a highly desirable student-faculty ratio, particularly if the student is skill-deficient and the institution is seriously interested in doing something about it. Lacking that favorable situation, comprehensive learning assistance programs in community colleges can and do provide an effective response to the dual problems of dealing with skill-deficient learners and functionally illiterate adults.

Providing learning assistance services is clearly an obligation of the community college. The other side of the coin is an equally important obligation to insist on unequivocal standards of achievement for all students in all disciplines. Creating an expectation of success is an important part of the teaching/learning process. Failure to equip both student and teacher with the skills needed to achieve those expectations is unconscionable.

References

Barshis, D. *Assisting Student Learning*. Los Angeles: Center for the Study of Community Colleges, 1984. 6 pp. (ED 251 139)

Bender, L. W., and Lukenbill, M. D. "Let's Begin with Ourselves." *Community and Junior College Journal*, 1984, *55* (2), 16-18.

Boylan, H. R. *Underpreparedness: A Reinterpretation of the Problem and Some Recommendations for Resolution*. Position Paper No. 1. Chicago: New Directions Task Force, National Association for Developmental Education, 1985.

Carbone, G. J., and Torgerson, A. *A Learning Assistance Support System for the Washington Community College System*. Olympia: Washington State Board for Community College Education, 1983. 13 pp. (ED 246 942)

Cramer, R., and Liberty, L. *A Plan for Improving Instruction and Services for Developmental Skills Students at Fresno City College*. Fresno, Calif.: Fresno City College, 1981. 72 pp. (ED 207 656)

Flamm, A. L., and others. *Reading Area Community College Basic Skills Program Review*. Reading, Pa.: Reading Area Community College, 1984. 77 pp. (ED 251 129)

Friedlander, J. *Innovative Approaches to Delivering Academic Assistance to Students*. Los Angeles: Center for the Study of Community Colleges, 1982. 20 pp. (ED 220 172)

Morante, E. A., and others. *Report to the Board of Higher Education of Results of the New Jersey Basic Skills Placement Testing and Recommendations on Instruction and Curriculum*. Trenton: New Jersey State Board of Higher Education, 1982. 54 pp. (ED 232 716)

New Jersey State Department of Higher Education. *Report on the Character of Remedial Programs in New Jersey Public Colleges and Universities. Fall 1984*. Trenton: New Jersey Basic Skills Council, New Jersey State Department of Higher Education, 1985. 107 pp. (ED 269 058)

Noel, L., Levitz, R., and Kaufman, J. "Campus Services for Academically Underprepared Students: A Report of a National Survey." In L. Noel and R. Levitz (eds.), *How to Succeed with Academically Underprepared Students: A Catalog of Successful Practices*. Ames, Iowa: American College Testing Program, 1982.

Palmer, J. C. "Do College Courses Improve Basic Reading and Writing Skills?" *Community College Review*, 1984, *12* (2), 20-28.

Roueche, J. E. "Between a Rock and a Hard Place." *Community and Junior College Journal*, 1984, *54* (7), 21-24.

Stumhofer, N. C. "The Role of the Admissions Office in the Academic Intervention and Support Program." Paper presented at the Annual National Conference of the National Association for Remedial/Developmental Studies in Postsecondary Education, Philadelphia, March 1984. 12 pp. (ED 253 273)

Washington State Board for Community College Education. *Platform for Excellence: A Review and Projection of Basic Skills, Developmental and Learning Support Education. Task Force Reports from the Learning Assistance Support System Project*. Olympia: Washington State Board for Community College Education, 1983. 52 pp. (ED 238 499)

Gilbert J. Carbone is assistant director for policy and special products, State Board for Community College Education, Olympia, Washington.

Assessment and placement systems go beyond testing; they are directly related to student success and satisfaction.

Assessment and Placement of Developmental and High-Risk Students

Dorothy Bray

Assessment systems are playing a critical role in college plans to improve student success. Assessment and placement activities have become increasingly valued as strategies that help colleges to deal with the wide range of learning and teaching problems of a diverse student clientele. Many students lack basic academic skills in the areas of reading, writing, and mathematics that they need if they are to succeed in college classes. My purpose is to describe the assessment and placement of high-risk and developmental education students.

Developmental education students are students who need assistance in overcoming skill deficiencies. Depending on the college, these underprepared students are known as *remedial, developmental, high-risk, lowachieving,* or *disadvantaged.* Identification of these students is generally based on current composite scores in mathematics, reading, or English tests coupled with information on study habits, attitudes, and goals.

Five key precepts underlie the relationship between assessment and developmental instruction: First, the relationship between assessment and instruction is becoming essential. Second, a comprehensive assessment and placement system establishes mutual goals with counseling, instruc-

K. M. Ahrendt (ed.). *Teaching the Developmental Education Student.*
New Directions for Community Colleges, no. 57. San Francisco: Jossey-Bass, Spring 1987.

tion, and research. Third, a critical path of assessment and placement activities provides a framework for student information. Fourth, research on assessment can provide a basis for decision making. Fifth, student flow through the institution is a key factor in planning for assessment use.

Since little history or tradition is available, some of the examples in this chapter are derived from the base of experiences at Sacramento City College, Sacramento, California. I will describe organizational concepts at this college, along with the uses that it makes of assessment and its assessment and placement practices.

Background

Four major trends are affecting the work of colleges with developmental education and high-risk students. First, a majority of college students have deficiencies in one or more areas of reading, writing, and mathematics skills. Second, colleges, universities, and industry are requiring increasingly higher skills competencies. Third, the remediation of basic skills is a fast-growing area within the curriculum. Fourth, most colleges identify developmental students by assessing the skills levels of entering freshmen.

Improving the literacy skills of all postsecondary education students is a prominent theme in the current literature. A 1983 national survey of colleges (Lederman, Ryzewic, and Ribaudo, 1983) found that 85 percent of the respondents perceived poor preparation to be a problem among incoming freshmen. A substantial percentage of all college freshmen required assistance in basic skills (28 percent in reading, 31 percent in writing, and 32 percent in mathematics), while a majority of the institutions surveyed offered basic skills courses (80 percent offered reading and mathematics, and 90 percent offered writing courses).

Evangelauf (1985) notes that 23 percent of the freshmen at two-year colleges and 17 percent of the freshman at four-year institutions took remedial writing. By 1983–1984, 60 percent of the students entering the California State University system failed to demonstrate entry-level writing competence on an English placement test, and 53 percent failed to demonstrate competence on a mathematics entry test.

Morante and others (1982) describe the nature of underprepared students in New Jersey. The New Jersey College Basic Skills Placement Test was instituted in 1978 as a proficiency examination measuring the reading, writing, and mathematics skills of students entering college. In spring and summer 1982, 51,135 students at New Jersey's state and county colleges and at ten independent colleges took the test. Of these students, 27 percent appeared to be proficient in verbal skills, 32 percent were proficient in computation skills, and only 11 percent were proficient in elementary algebra.

Assessment and Student Success

Two key questions are, How can community colleges be both effective and efficient with large numbers of underprepared students? and, What assists underprepared students to be more successful? In many community colleges, the assessment of students' basic skills in reading, writing, and mathematics and the placement of these students in courses that are appropriate to their skills levels have become key strategies for improving student success. The emphasis is, first, on increasingly systematic basic skills assessment that provides data on students' learning needs; second, on directing and placing students in appropriate levels of classes; and, third, on establishing a system of accountability for student learning and retention for courses, programs, and degree completion.

The theme of assessment and its relationship to student success is receiving increasing attention throughout postsecondary education. A report from the National Institute of Education (1984) describes assessment and feedback as constituting one of the three critical conditions for the achievement of excellence. That report states that the use of assessment information to redirect institutional efforts is an essential ingredient in effective learning and that it serves as a powerful level for student involvement.

Roueche (1984b, p. 6) indicates that mandatory assessment and placement are strong contributors to student success: "Institutions are no longer able or willing to use the high school grade point averages as indicators of student ability or true performance. They are more likely to use standardized tests—for example, SAT, ACT—as measures of student potential (without interventions) to be successful in college. Because these tests provide only indications of problems . . . , on-site testing for more targeted and in-depth analysis of these deficiencies is conducted during orientation and/or registration or once the student is enrolled in the developmental classes. Frequently, the tests are constructed through the joint efforts of developmental and representative freshman-level instructors as a means of validating actual skill levels required in follow-up courses."

Lederman, Ryzewic, and Ribaudo (1983) found in their survey that 97 percent of the responding institutions assessed the skills levels of entering freshmen; only 2 percent of the institutions held that assessment was unnecessary. A 1985 study conducted by the American College Testing Program and the American Association of Community and Junior Colleges (AACJC) reports that more than 75 percent of both urban and nonurban institutions require some form of testing or the submission of test scores from some or all entering students (American College Testing Program, 1985).

Richardson (1983) asserts that the open door of the community college too often becomes a revolving door when student needs are not met and program quality decreases. He indicates that a response by community colleges to the issue of open access should resolve questions related to defining the competencies needed for a reasonable chance of success in each program offered, assessing students to determine whether they have the requisite competencies, and placing them appropriately.

The Developing Relationship Between Assessment and Instruction

One emerging theme is that there is a significant link between the activities of assessment and instruction. Since a majority of community college students require developmental assistance in reading, writing, and mathematics, the goals and objectives of instruction have become increasingly dependent on assessment activities that monitor the growth of students from entrance to exit. The crucial relationship that is developing between assessment and instruction asks a new set of questions: How do assessment and appropriate placement improve learning and retention? How does the use of assessment affect college curriculum and services? What assessment tests are most appropriate for use in community colleges? What guidelines regarding assessment and placement should community colleges use? How do we integrate assessment and placement into the total college educational and student services program? How can assessment and placement data help community college faculty to improve their teaching and increase learning outcomes for students?

A broader definition of assessment has emerged that is linked to instructional improvement. In the past, students were tested and sent to existing courses. Little emphasis was placed on designing courses that would meet the needs that students demonstrated on the tests. Thus, testing was an isolated activity, often with negative implications. Now, assessment is being viewed as a process that identifies students' potential success levels, diagnoses their skills deficiencies, and provides a basis for a student plan for enrollment in courses and programs. In practice, assessment systems also have begun to serve two other purposes: to assist in the improvement of teaching and learning and to provide information for decisions on retention and advancement. This new definition of assessment points up the close interactive relationship between assessment, instruction, and student success, viewed as retention.

Assessment and placement systems go beyond testing. They have a close relationship to courses and programs. The mutual goals of assessment, placement, and instruction include successful student performance in class, successful completion of courses, student satisfaction, and improved teaching and learning.

A Comprehensive Assessment and Placement System

A model designed by the Learning, Assessment, Retention Consortium (LARC) of the California Community Colleges (1982) describes assessment and placement as consisting of four systems that involve all segments of the college. Each of the four activities of assessment, advisement, instruction, and follow-up has an information system. Based on an assessment and placement system, students are assessed. Based on guidance and placement systems, students are advised and placed. Based on a program delivery system, students are instructed. Based on a research system, student progress is followed up and evaluated. The LARC assessment and placement model depicted in Figure 1 illustrates the relationships between these four systems.

Nine assumptions serve as a foundation for the model: Assessment and placement should be an integral part of the total college instructional and student services programs. Assessment and placement should be supportive of students' educational goals rather than exclusionary. All college groups should be involved and informed about the purposes, effects, and procedures related to assessment and placement. Faculty should use assessment and placement to improve their teaching. Administrators should use assessment and placement to improve decisions about college programs. An institution's response to student objectives and interests will improve through the use of assessment and placement. Assessment does not screen students out; it screens them in. Assessment systems and instruments are not infallible. Random student placement is not educationally sound.

Besides clarifying the elements of a comprehensive assessment and placement system, the model includes operational guidelines. Different combinations of these guidelines allow for individual college decisions about philosophy, goals, objectives, and implementation. Figure 2 details the questions that colleges need to answer in establishing the assessment and placement system exemplified by the LARC model.

Figure 3 describes a program delivery system and operational definitions of key types of courses into which students are placed. The system depicted in Figure 3 was developed as a result of a statewide workshop of California community colleges in 1983. Figure 3 suggests that students can proceed from an assessment and placement process through two types of learning skills programs to preparatory programs and then to traditional academic and vocational programs. *Learning skills program* was suggested by workshop participants as an umbrella term for a process that will prepare students to succeed in college courses. Workshop participants defined two types of learning skills programs through which students might proceed: Remedial education programs are designed to help students to achieve fundamental learning skills necessary to meet the minimum expectations for college courses. Developmental education programs are designed to improve students' chances for success in college courses. In this system, learning skills courses can be credit or noncredit, depending on local definitions. It is possible, as the model suggests, for students to be assessed and proceed directly to preparatory courses (courses in such a sequence as Chemistry 1A followed by Chemistry 1B) and then on to academic or vocational programs.

Figure 1. LARC Consortium Assessment and Placement Model

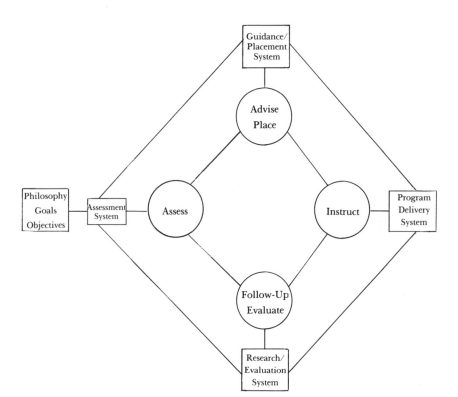

The premise that individual student success is closely related to an institution's ability to organize for directing the student to this success is important to the discussion. A central question is, Who is responsible for the success of the underprepared students, the institution or the student? Roueche (1984a) quotes Maxwell, who pointed out that patterns for underachievers are enduring; expectations for improvement, by themselves, are not enough. The situations that promote growth are situations that challenge and support the learner while linking remedial efforts to the student's regular curriculum. Even more pointedly, Roueche (1984b, p. 51) indicates, "processes employed to manage students are as important as, if not more important than, instructional processes."

Figure 2. Guidelines for the Development of an Assessment and Placement System

Systems	Who?	What?	How and Where?
Assessment	Who will be assessed? Who will do the assessing? Who will be administratively responsible?	What basic skills will be assessed and used to determine placement? How will cutoff scores be determined? What alternatives to standardized tests will be available?	How will an assessment and placement system differ from a diagnostic system? How will an assessment and placement system be used? How will the system be able to screen large numbers rapidly and inexpensively? How and where will testing take place?
Guidance and Placement	Who will do the advising? Who will be administratively responsible?	What are advising needs? What is the relationship of the advisory system to other support services?	How should advisory services be delivered? How should advisers be selected and trained? How are placement and information to be unified?
Program Delivery	Who will determine available programs? Who will be administratively responsible?	What courses will be available for skills placement? What minimum skill competencies are needed to succeed in courses?	How many courses and levels will be available? How will staff be trained?
Research and Evaluation	Who will conduct follow-up studies? Who will be administratively responsible?	What type of program evaluation will be conducted? What student progress information will be available?	How will research results be used to adjust placement as needed?

Figure 3. Program Delivery System

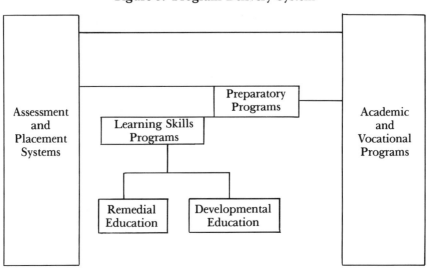

A Critical Path for Assessment and Placement

Three assessment stages make up a critical path for assessment and placement that will provide student intake information and student outcome data. Colleges are beginning to go beyond their emphasis on entry-level assessment to placement into courses. Once the student has been assessed and placed and the student has received instruction, his or her movement from the entry-level course to another course has prompted a broadening of assessment and placement activities and considerations.

The measurement of performance at three important reference points as the student moves through the institution suggests that there is a triad of assessment activities: entry-level assessment, exit measurement from courses, degree or certificate measurement on completion of programs. Each activity provides information that guides instruction of the student through various developmental stages. This information provides a framework for directing student flow. Rather than allowing students to place themselves, students are guided to learning situations in which they demonstrate the basic skills needed in order to succeed.

The first stage, entry-level assessment, is generally a sorting process that develops an index of student skills that can be used to guide student placement into courses. Many community colleges have developed this stage as a process that produces multifaceted information that includes demographic information, basic skills information, description of the student's personal goals, requests for academic assistance, and a matching of the student's goals and expectations with courses as components of the student's college plan. This information is used to certify student skills competencies and to identify any needs for remedial intervention as well as to identify opportunity for advanced or accelerated work.

The second stage, exit measurement, focuses on the assessment of learning that occurs in the skills development courses. At this stage, assessment takes the form of exercises demonstrating the development of certain competencies. The resulting information describes the student's readiness to go to the next step or level of learning. Several techniques have been used for exit measurement. Pre- and posttesting—use of the same test to measure skills at course entry and exit—is often required in reading courses. Instructor evaluation of students' in-class progress is another form of exit assessment from courses. The demonstration of proficiencies as by a written essay in a writing course is still another example of exit measurement. Exit measurement as a form of the rapidly growing field of outcomes assessment is of growing interest to decision makers who are seeking to connect funding issues to performance growth of students in colleges.

The third stage, degree measurement, is based on exit criteria from the college or program. It matches the student's performance with a standard that designates or certifies that the student has developed and demonstrated certain skills. Competency performance in the areas of reading, writing, and mathematics are areas that are often measured. Roueche (1984a) found that more than half of all college institutional groups administered exit tests in three basic skills areas.

This triad of activities indicates that a significant institutional shift is occurring. Rather than using assessment just to control entry to programs, institutions are now using assessment to focus on students' learning achievement. This dual emphasis on entry assessment and outcomes assessment suggests an emerging need to consider placement entry standards simultaneously with exit standards.

Campus Studies

A review of the current literature from the community college field reveals that documented college experiences with entry-level assessment are diverse but still relatively rare. Generally, colleges first have engaged in the experience of using assessment and then have looked at some of its impact on students and the institution. The literature consists largely of responses to five types of questions: How well does a standardized test predict student readiness, particularly in composition? What is the impact of entry-level assessment procedures on curriculum, services, and minority students? How successful were students who followed the placement recommendations? How effective is mandatory assessment and placement, and how effective is advisory assessment and placement? Are students being properly placed as a result of assessment?

There is little unanimity in the responses. Several colleges have reported that standardized tests do predict student readiness. Olson and Martin (1980) found than an objective test was the single best predictor of credit English grades. Santa Rosa Junior College (1984) found that scores on the reading test correlated significantly with students' overall grade point averages. Boggs (1984) found that the TASK instrument from the Stanford Test of Academic Skills seemed more effective in increasing student achievement in developmental writing than in freshman composition but that assessment by writing sample seemed to be particularly effective in increasing achievement in developmental writing. Rasor and Powell (1984) found no correlation in using a placement test consisting of vocabulary and usage subtests for placement in composition. Haase and Magee (1983) found the reading test to be a significant predictor of grades in composition.

Some colleges are beginning to document the success of students who follow placement recommendations. Haase and Caffrey (1984) found that students who availed themselves of the established assessment, advisement, and placement process had retention rates ranging between 61 and 77 percent, while students who used other processes had success rates ranging from 44 to 66 percent. The effectiveness of mandatory assessment and placement is verified by Bers (1982), who found that, under mandatory placement, the percentage of enrollees in college composition who successfully completed the courses increased over the levels reported under advisory placement the year before.

Proper placement as a result of assessment was verified by Cordrey (1984), who found that misplacement rates were small in some areas: 9.3 percent in writing, 6.2 percent in reading, 1 percent in composition, and 33.4 percent in algebra. Haase and Magee (1983) found that students were properly placed in their English courses as verified through assessment, promotion rates, or both. Nationally, colleges express a stronger commitment to mandatory assessment than they do to mandatory placement (Roueche, 1984a). For example, while 81 percent of the major research universities stated that preassessment of writing skills was required, only 58 percent stated that placement into writing courses was mandatory.

Student Flow from Assessment Through Instruction

A key consideration in planning for the use of assessment is the issue of student flow. The model described in this section is based on developmental education programs at Sacramento City College, Sacramento, California. The model depicts the logical order in which the student moves through the assessment and placement process to instruction and through exit measurement from the course. The model is college-specific; it is not meant to suggest a standard.

The model represents the student characteristics of those enrolling in two developmental areas: composition and reading. The definition of the developmental student comes from his or her individual assessment profile. The model also describes the institutional programs designed for the student. The activities described here have evolved over a period of seven years as the college has undertaken to develop responses to underprepared students. The activities are grouped in the order in which the student is assigned to instruction. Some of the activities are better defined than others, since the college is continually adjusting the system described here.

How do we apply assessment to the instructional setting? Figure 4 depicts an overall flow path for students at Sacramento City College, beginning with entry assessment activities and culminating in degree assessment activities. In this model, entry assessment is made up of three kinds of information. This information is synthesized and then used to prepare a composite profile for the students.

In Figure 4, the student participates in entry-level assessment, which produces a student profile plan containing three kinds of information: student plans, personal history, and proficiency criteria based on test scores. This information is used at orientation sessions where course and program advising take place and appropriate courses are selected. Entry into courses is determined by student selection, prerequisite criteria, or both. A unique linkage between assessment and instruction is depicted in the activity of demand scheduling, where courses can be added or dropped based on student needs as identified in assessment.

Once students are in courses, reassessment of initial placement generally takes place as diagnostic information is gathered based on writing samples or other types of exercises. More advising of students takes place here, and students can be reassigned to alternate classes if they are not placed in appropriate courses. Through a continuing program review process, the curriculum content of the skills courses is matched to the needs described in student profiles. Students complete the courses and, where required, participate in the exit assessment, which verifies their competency gains. Finally, the degree assessment information yields a measurement of a student's skills according to college- or district-determined standards. The arrows in Figure 4 indicate that students may advance or repeat until they demonstrate the designated mastery of skills.

The flow model depicted in Figure 4 is organized to respond to six questions: What type of student, based on assessed proficiency abilities, is assigned to each of the three designated levels of instruction in reading and writing? What kind of reading competencies should be demonstrated? How do instructors verify student placement? How does the curriculum content match the defined academic deficiencies of the students assigned to a given level of instruction? What skills does the student need in order to exit from the course? What skills does the student need to demonstrate in order to earn an A.A. degree?

Figure 4. Student Flow at Sacramento City College

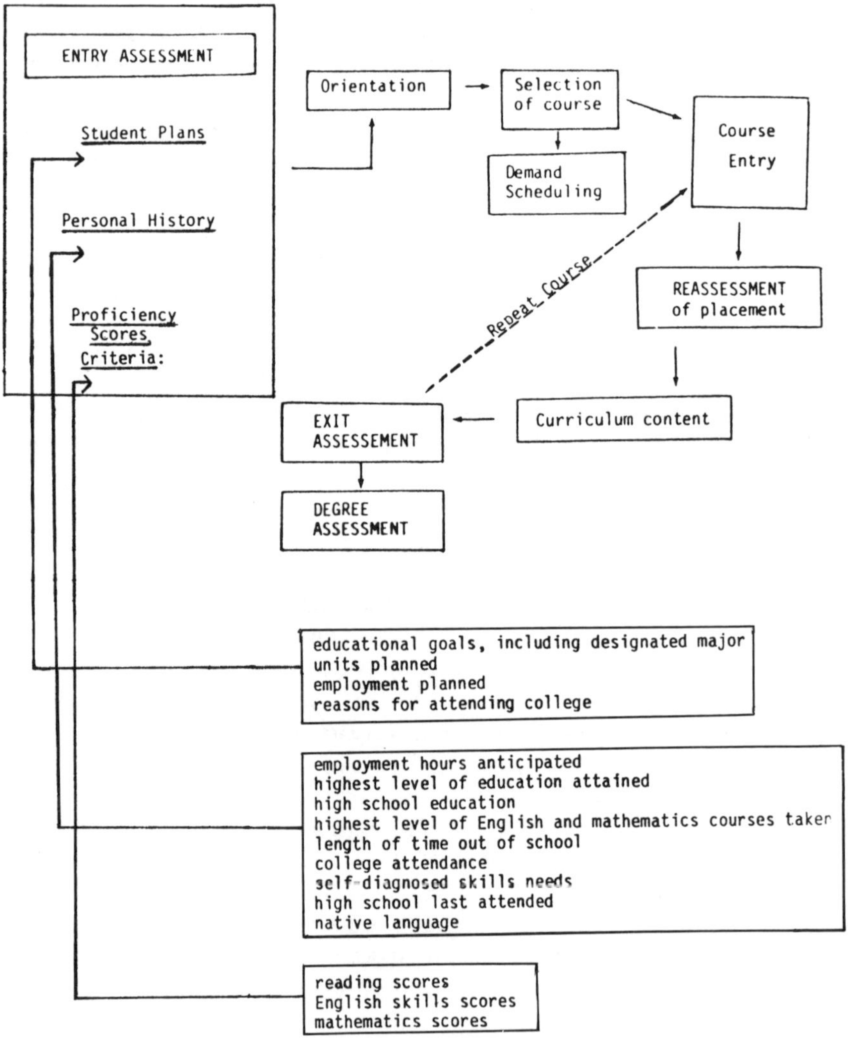

Eight assumptions underlie the model: A standardized test is a good predictor of reading ability, but it is recognized that there will be exceptions to placement by scores on standardized tests. Instructor recommendations are used to augment assessment data; they may make recommendations regarding the student flow both into and out of the courses. There is a connection between reading abilities and success in composition courses. The competency profile for student placement in levels was developed by consensus of the staff. The student movement into and out of the courses is based on criteria to which faculty agree and which they apply somewhat uniformly. The exit assessment profile and criteria were agreed upon by consensus. Placement is based on raw scores related to grade level by a national norming process. Levels are periodically adjusted as demonstrated by need. English courses are not the only areas of developmental training.

Conclusion

In this chapter, I have examined the use of assessment for high-risk and developmental students. A necessary relationship between assessment and developmental instruction has emerged whereby assessment provides crucial information about the student at various stages in his or her flow through the college. In this concluding section, I will consider the future of assessment at community colleges.

Not only colleges but decision makers are now taking an interest in assessment. It is important to note that activities related to assessment are in a stage of development and that they provide a basis for an ongoing, vigorous effort to improve student success and retention. As a result of this interest, assessment will continue to be a major fiscal, political, and educational issue throughout the remainder of this century. Despite phobias against testing as discriminatory, unscientific, and imperfect, assessment of students will increase over the next ten years. Students will become more proactive about assessment programs, and as a result, student goals will need to become an integral part of assessment processes.

The concept of assessment has been decisively redefined. A redefinition of assessment as a comprehensive process of testing, advising, placement, and follow-up will continue to allow assessment to become a total institutional process and an all-college support model. A key motif will be collaboration, not competition. Growing partnerships between test makers and institutions will provide for research, analysis, and staff development services and support in return for use of a test product. Increased cooperation between high schools and colleges in sharing assessment, placement, and follow-up information will be one of the most important developments of the 1980s.

Models for the organization of assessment and placement activities will continue to change rapidly. The current model, which uses assessment to place students in courses within an institution, will be replaced with a model using assessment in a continuum proceeding from entry to exit and follow-up. Student services and instruction will become coequal providers of testing and advisory services. Community outreach assessment and advising centers are already being developed by many colleges. Mobile vans are being used to take assessment to the community.

Colleges expect to adopt tougher assessment prerequisites mandating increasing numbers of students to participate in the analysis of their skills abilities. One of the most difficult tasks that institutions will face will be to connect skills deficiencies uncovered by assessment with course instruction and with learning and teaching success. A continuous flow of information on students from assessment, placement, and follow-up will be a catalyst to efforts to define and improve the quality of learning programs as student and course matches and mismatches are analyzed.

The amount of money that is spent on test instruments will be less relevant than the amount spent on a continuous advising and follow-up system of information. At the same time, the technology of assessment will continue to develop rapidly around increasingly sophisticated computer-based data retrieval systems. The selection of assessment instruments will involve several criteria: Comparative data, although they will continue to be sought after by groups external to colleges, will not be as informative as aggregate data. A variety of assessment instruments will be less important than single instruments that are capable of providing various levels of information. Local, institutional tests will prove inadequate compared to professional tests with flexible norms geared to local student characteristics. Technological innovations in testing include a program of computer-based diagnostic testing developed by the College Board and the Educational Testing Service. Diagnostic testing, in combination with computerized adaptive placement testing, will provide increasingly individualized information.

Finally, assessment will become the nexus where education and work can meet. A model emphasizing assessment, placement, and follow-up will facilitate a student's movement through college as well as the movement from school to work. Assessment, training information, placement services, and follow-up information will be used to maximize the match between employee and job. Assessment will lessen some of the problems of job dissatisfaction through accurate identification of worker skills and an improved fit between person and job. Applied to employment, assessment will allow differentiation among the underskilled, the unskilled, and the overskilled employee. Entry-level assessment will be connected to career advisement.

If, as this forecast suggests, the present can serve as a prologue to the future, then assessment systems will continue to emerge as key institutional support and student success models. Most colleges now using assessment systems are noting that a majority of their students are more successful than they were five years ago, whatever the assessment model utilized. Clearly, assessment influences student success, and it has led to the development of a new partnership between institutions and students. We know more about critical skills competencies, we use this information to improve success in learning and teaching, and we are becoming increasingly successful in teaching and learning.

References

American College Testing Program. *ACT and AACJC to Cooperate in National Surveys of Community, Junior, and Technical Colleges.* Iowa City, Iowa: American College Testing Program, 1985.

Bers, T. H. *Assessment of Mandatory Placement in Communications: Fall 1981.* Des Plaines, Ill.: Office of Institutional Research, Oakton Community College, 1982. 18 pp. (ED 214 599)

Boggs, G. R. *The Effect of Basic Skills Assessment on Student Achievement and Persistence at Butte College: A Research Report.* Oroville, Calif.: Butte College, 1984. 23 pp. (ED 244 686)

Cordrey, L. J. *Evaluation of the Skills Prerequisite Systems at Fullerton College (A Two-Year Follow-Up).* Fullerton, Calif.: Fullerton College, 1984. 99 pp. (ED 244 663)

Evangelauf, J. "Enrollment in Remedial Courses Jumps at 63 Percent of Colleges That Offer Them." *Chronicle of Higher Education,* February 13, 1985, p. 3.

Haase, M. H., and Caffrey, P. *The Impact of a Coordinated Assessment/Placement Process on Student Success and Retention: Statistical Response to a Grant Proposal.* Sacramento, Calif.: Sacramento City College, 1984. 27 pp. (ED 243 540)

Haase, M. H., and Magee, S. *A Statistical Evaluation of the Efficacy of Selected English Courses.* Sacramento, Calif.: Sacramento City College, 1983. 15 pp. (ED 231 421)

Learning, Assessment, Retention Consortium of California Community Colleges. *Assessment/Placement Model: A Monograph.* Sacramento: Learning Assessment, Retention Consortium of California Community Colleges, 1982.

Lederman, M., Ryzewic, S., and Ribaudo, M. *Assessment and Improvement of the Academic Skills of Entering Freshman Students: A National Survey.* Research Monograph Series Report No. 5. New York: Instructional Resources Center, Office of Academic Affairs, City University of New York, 1983.

Morante, E. A., and others. *Report to the Board of Higher Education on Results of the New Jersey College Basic Skills Placement Testing and Recommendations on Instruction and Curriculum.* Trenton: New Jersey Basic Skills Council, New Jersey State Board of Higher Education, 1982. 54 pp. (ED 232 716)

National Institute of Education. *Involvement in Learning: Realizing the Potential of American Higher Education. Final Report of the Study Group on the Conditions of Excellence in American Higher Education.* Washington, D.C.: National Institute of Education, 1984. 127 pp. (ED 246 833)

Olson, M. A., and Martin, D. "Assessment of Entering Student Writing Skills in the Community College." Paper presented at the Annual Meeting of the American Educational Research Association, Boston, April 7-11, 1980. 35 pp. (ED 235 845)

Rasor, R. A., and Powell, T. *Predicting English Writing Course Success with the Vocabulary and Usage Subtests of the Descriptive Tests of Language Skills of the*

College Board. Sacramento, Calif.: American River College, 1984. 34 pp. (ED 243 535)

Richardson, R. C., Jr. *Future of the Open Door*. Paper presented at the Annual Convention of the Association of Community College Trustees, Phoenix, Ariz., October 1983. 8 pp. (ED 235 848)

Roueche, J. E. *College Response to Low-Achieving Students. A National Survey*. Orlando, Fla.: HBJ Media Systems, 1984a.

Roueche, J. E. "Literacy Needs and Developments in American Community Colleges." Paper presented at the National Adult Literacy Conference, Washington, D.C., January 19-20, 1984b. 14 pp. (ED 240 291)

Santa Rosa Junior College. *DRT/ASSET/Final Grade Study Fund for Instructional Improvement Final Report, 1983-1984*. Santa Rosa, Calif.: Santa Rosa Junior College, 1984. 189 pp. (ED 253 272)

Dorothy Bray is vice-president at the College of the Desert in Palm Springs, California.

Community colleges face a new challenge: to provide appropriate instruction and services to learning-disabled students.

Learning Disabilities and the Developmental Education Program

Bonnie J. Young, Bonnie L. Staebler

The years between 1975 and 1985 can be described as a decade of dignity for learning-disabled students. In 1975, Congress passed the Education for All Handicapped Children Act; in 1977, the regulations for Section 504 of the Vocational Rehabilitation Act were signed; and in 1981, the Rehabilitation Services added learning disabilities to its list of recognized handicaps. According to the U.S. Department of Education, the number of learning-disabled students identified between the years 1976 and 1984 increased by 127 percent. In fact, according to the U.S. General Accounting Office, nearly two million school-age students were provided with special education under the learning-disabled category in 1981 (National Information Center for Handicapped Children and Youth, 1985). Many students within this group are seeking further educational opportunities in developmental education programs at the community college level.

A survey by the Vocational Committee of the Association for Children and Adults with Learning Disabilities (Association for Children and Adults with Learning Disabilities, 1982) revealed that 14 percent of the adult learning-disabled population had tried a two-year or four-year college, 32 percent were currently in college, 4 percent had graduated from a

K. M. Ahrendt (ed.). *Teaching the Developmental Education Student.*
New Directions for Community Colleges, no. 57. San Francisco: Jossey-Bass, Spring 1987.

junior college, 9 percent had earned a bachelor's degree, and 8 percent had earned or were earning a postgraduate degree. The influx of learning-disabled adults into the college setting documented by these figures has created a need for additional services.

In 1984, a survey of 106 California community colleges (Ostertag and Baker, 1984) revealed that more than 80 percent of the colleges had formal programs for learning-disabled students; another 12 percent provided informal services. Methods for meeting the needs of this population included special classes, tutorial support, counseling, and other auxiliary services. Individual Education Plans (IEPs) were maintained on more than 91 percent of the learning disabled who received services from formal programs.

Community colleges are particularly attractive to the learning-disabled adult because they usually provide testing and career counseling; tutoring in basic subjects; adult education and GED training; liberal arts courses and opportunities for transfer to a four-year school; developmental education in reading, mathematics, written language, and vocabulary; and vocational assessment and occupational programs. These services have always been available. The challenge today is to adapt them to the needs of learning-disabled students. Consequently, community college faculty are asking three questions: Who are the learning-disabled students? What kinds of services should be provided? and What informational resources are available?

Who Are the Learning Disabled?

The term *learning disability* came into use in the early 1960s. Previously, such terms as *brain damage, minimal brain dysfunction, word blindness,* and *perceptual handicap* were used to describe the problem. In 1968, the National Advisory Committee on Handicapped Children developed a definition that was later included in Public Law 94-142. The definition described a learning disability "as a disorder in one or more of the basic psychological processes involved in understanding or in using language, spoken or written, which may manifest itself in an imperfect ability to listen, think, speak, read, write, spell, or do mathematical calculations. The term includes such conditions as perceptual handicaps, brain injury, minimal brain dysfunction, dyslexia, and developmental aphasia. The term does not include children who have learning problems which are primarily the result of visual, hearing, or motor handicaps, of mental retardation, of emotional disturbance, environmental, cultural, or economic disadvantage" (Kirk, 1968, p. 34). This definition had legal status since it was included in P.L. 94-142 and in the laws and regulations of most states.

Another definition was developed by the National Joint Committee for Learning Disabilities (NJCLD) in 1981. The NJCLD was comprised of representatives from the American Speech-Language-Hearing Association (ASHA), the Association for Children and Adults with Learning Disabilities (ACLD), the Council for Learning Disabilities (CLD), the Division for Children with Communication Disorders (DCCD), the International Reading Association (IRA), and the Orton Dyslexia Society. The new definition stated that *learning disabilities* was a generic term that referred to a heterogeneous group of disorders manifested by significant difficulties in the acquisition and use of listening, speaking, reading, writing, reasoning, or mathematical abilities. These disorders were intrinsic to the individual, and they were presumed to be due to dysfunction of the central nervous system. "Even though a learning disability may occur concomitantly with other handicapping conditions (for example, sensory impairment, mental retardation, social and emotional disturbance) or environmental influences (for example, cultural differences, insufficient/inappropriate instruction, psychogenic factors), it is not the direct result of those conditions or influences" (Hammill, Leigh, McNutt, and Larsen, 1981, p. 336). Under this definition, the emphasis moved from single disorders to heterogeneous groups of disorders. This action emphasized the absolutely critical need for careful diagnosis to determine the nature of the disability. The category was so broad that effective treatment was impossible without accurate diagnosis.

The new definition recognized the broad basis for a learning disability, but it did not emphasize the lasting nature of the disability. It was not until 1984 that the Association for Children and Adults with Learning Disabilities passed a resolution recognizing that learning disability did not disappear once a student left public school. According to that resolution, specific learning disabilities were a chronic condition of presumed neurological origin that selectively interfered with the development, integration, and demonstration of verbal and nonverbal abilities. Specific learning disabilities exist as a distinct handicapping condition in the presence of average to superior intelligence, adequate sensory and motor systems, and adequate learning opportunities. The condition varies in its manifestations and in the degree of severity. It can affect self-esteem, education, vocation, socialization, and daily living activities (Association for Children and Adults with Learning Disabilities, 1984). This resolution provided a definition of the term *learning disabilities* that stressed the potential of the disability for affecting people throughout their lives. It helped to create a momentum across the nation. Increasing numbers of learning-disabled students began to attend community college. Selected organizations and self-help groups came into being. And, community college faculties began asking questions about treatment that required an understanding of the various subcategories of learning disabilities.

In applying the various definitions of learning disabilities at the public school level, school district personnel have typically held fast to two elements without the various subcategories. First, there must be a discrepancy between intelligence and achievement; second, there must be low performance in a basic skill area, such as reading, mathematics, or written language. However, public school officials have been reluctant to establish restrictive eligibility criteria. Research has repeatedly pointed out that many students identified as learning disabled do not exhibit the characteristics specified under P.L. 94–142 (Shepard, Smith, and Vojir, 1983; Algozzine and Ysseldyke, 1983). In fact, Algozzine and Ysseldyke (1983) reported that as many as sixty different definitions or criteria were used in identifying the learning disabled. The guidelines established in 1984 by the National Task Force on Identifying Learning Disabled included the recommendation that basic psychological processing deficits should be used as an indicator for the determination of eligibility (Chalfant, 1985). The International Academy for Research in Learning Disabilities (Keogh, Major-Kingsley, Omori-Gordon, and Reid, 1982) identified eight process deficit areas: *Activity level* refers to hypoactive or hyperactive levels of activity, such as facing away or acting out. *Attention* refers to the ability to focus on a task over a period of time. Attentional deficits are often associated with distractibility. *Auditory perception* refers to the understanding of information that is heard. Auditory perception includes such components as auditory discrimination, blending, and listening comprehension. *Fine motor coordination* refers to the use of the small muscles with visual perception in such activities as handwriting, copying, and drawing. *Gross motor coordination* refers to the use of large muscle groups. Such activities as jumping, running, and throwing are examples of gross motor abilities. *Memory* refers to the ability to store and retrieve information. Short- and long-term memory, free recall, sequencing, and incidental learning are all examples of memory abilities. *Oral language* refers to the comprehension and production of verbal material. Vocabulary, semantics, and syntax are common oral language processes. *Visual perception* refers to the ability to understand information that is seen. Visual perception includes such components as matching, discrimination, and spatial relations.

The International Academy for Research in Learning Disabilities did much for the field of learning disabilities. By recognizing the components of learning disabilities across national cultures, its work made research in learning disabilities much more feasible. For example, Lyon (1985) reported preliminary findings regarding the subtypes of learning disabilities and reading instruction. His research indicated that certain reading instructional approaches may be beneficial for certain subtypes and harmful for others.

With all the complexities in the field of learning disabilities, it becomes imperative for community college faculty to set their own policy, criteria, and procedures regarding the identification of the learning-disabled student.

What Services Should Be Provided?

As already noted, community colleges have many services already in place that can be extended to learning-disabled students. The majority of the extension must occur within the developmental education program. For example, most community colleges provide academic skill testing through their developmental education program. The assessment that such programs provide must be extended to individualized basic skill testing and individualized process testing.

Assessment. Individualized skill testing should include norm-referenced achievement tests, such as the Woodcock Reading Mastery Tests (Woodcock, 1981) and the Keymath Diagnostic Arithmetic Test (Connolly, Nachtman, and Pritchett, 1976). Criterion-referenced tests should also be included. The Brigance Inventory of Essential Skills (Brigance, 1981) includes useful subtests that can be used to assess basic sight vocabulary, functional math skills, map-reading skills, and reading comprehension levels. Informal skills tests can be developed from tasks required of the student in specific courses. For example, if the student is experiencing difficulty with a personal finance class, the curriculum of the course can be used to develop test items.

Process areas must also be assessed. Typically, assessment of process areas includes learning styles; input channels, such as auditory and visual perception; and output channels, such as written expression, oral expression, or fine motor skills. Formal and informal measures can be applied. The formal tests of learning style include the Learning Styles Inventory (Dunn, Dunn, and Price, 1985), the Learning Style Inventory (Kolb, 1976), and the Cognitive Style Interest Inventory (Hill, 1971).

Auditory and visual perception can be formally assessed by the Detroit Tests of Learning Aptitude (Hammill, 1985), the Auditory Discrimination Test, Revised (Wepman, 1975), the Visual Discrimination Test (Wepman, 1976a), the Visual Memory Test (Wepman, 1976b), the Benton Visual Retention Test (Benton, 1956), and the Goldman-Fristoe-Woodcock Auditory Test Battery (Goldman, Fristoe, and Woodcock, 1974). In addition, administration and examination of several subtests on the Wechsler Adult Intelligence Scale, Revised (Wechsler, 1981) can yield supportive documentation. For example, a student who is having difficulty with auditory memory may find it particularly difficult to score well on the digit span or arithmetic subtests. Conversely, a student who is having difficulty with visual perception may find it particularly difficult to score well on the block design or object assembly subtests.

Although it is relatively difficult to substantiate informal methods of assessing a student's learning style and perceptual processes, the experienced diagnostician can glean much from observational data. Watching how a student goes about a certain task, asking a student how a particular problem is being solved, or becoming particularly involved in the teaching-learning situation constantly yields information helpful to the diagnostic process. Lerner (1976) points out that diagnosis must be constantly updated by data derived from the treatment implemented. Such information is helpful in identifying how a student is attempting to learn. Instructors should use such knowledge in designing instructional techniques. It is not recommended that they spend any time trying to remediate basic psychological processes in adults.

In addition to the input channels, a student's output channels, such as written expression, oral expression, and fine motor skills, should be assessed if the student has been experiencing difficulty in these areas. Formal assessment in written expression can use the Test of Written Language (Hammill and Larsen, 1978) or the Test of Written Spelling (Larsen and Hammill, 1976). Informal methods for conducting such assessment include task-specific evaluation. For example, for the student who is experiencing difficulty in writing a research paper, it is appropriate to analyze the student's writing style or the paper's structure to determine where the student's learning process is breaking down.

In regard to oral expression, several formal assessment measures can be helpful. The Peabody Picture Vocabulary Test, Revised (Dunn and Dunn, 1981) helps to determine the age equivalency of the student's receptive vocabulary. Another useful formal measure is the mean length of the student's utterances. Listening to the student, the diagnostician can also judge the complexity of the student's sentence structure, the student's use of modifiers, and the student's concept level in oral language.

Finally, fine motor response can be examined informally. Is the student's cursive writing legible? Can the student use a typewriter or a word processor effectively?

Tutoring. Tutoring is another area of service that needs to be extended within developmental education programs. In the past, tutoring has consisted basically of helping the student to understand the material in a textbook, helping the student to finish an assignment for class, or both. However, if the student has a diagnosed perceptual learning disability, the tutor may need to present the material in ways that will maximize the student's learning strengths while minimizing the student's learning weaknesses. For example, a demonstration of the concept to be learned may be more effective than a discussion of the concept. That is, the student who assembles a pizza following the principles of division of labor may come to understand the concept far better than the student who merely discusses it with a tutor.

New Instructional Strategies. Remedial instruction is the third area of service that needs to be extended within developmental education programs. At present, remedial instruction often occurs in large groups, and it is scheduled and assigned by functional level. The teacher's only knowledge of the student's ability is a grade level for the basic skills being taught. Now, the teacher will be given assessment information specific to each student regarding how the student learns, how the student processes information, and how the skill can best be taught. Remedial teaching requires individual or small-group instruction. The use of peer tutors and community volunteers helps to reduce the demands on the instructor.

As an alternative to the remedial approach taken by most developmental education programs, the instructional strategy approach can be implemented for adult learning-disabled students. Alley and Deshler (1979) pointed out that teaching a student how to learn is perhaps of greater value than teaching a student what to learn. The instructional strategy approach is characterized by teaching the student to cope with the learning environment in new ways. For example, a student might ask an instructor to accept a photo essay rather than a written essay as a means for demonstrating that learning has occurred. Teaching a student how to perform a task analysis is another example.

Independent Living Skills. Another area that must be added to any developmental program for the adult learning-disabled student is assistance with independent living skills. Living skills, such as reading bus schedules, shopping, preparing meals, and managing money, must not be taken for granted. Learning-disabled students do not always generalize skills learned in one setting to other settings in which the same skills are required. An overview of the problems of transition from school to work is highlighted by Smith-Davis (1983). A program called Project Independence was developed to provide a daily living skill curriculum. It was first implemented in 1983 by the New York Association for Children and Adults with Learning Disabilities (New York Association for Children and Adults with Learning Disabilities, 1983).

Advocacy. Advocacy for the student with other faculty is the fifth area that must be extended within the developmental education program. The information about how a particular student learns must be made available to other faculty and developed on the basis of recommendations regarding instructional practices. Several methods for accomplishing this task can be explored. For example, the developmental education faculty member who assesses the student can give the assessment to the guidance counselor, who can then advocate on behalf of the student with other faculty. The developmental education faculty member can act directly with other faculty members on the student's behalf. And last, the developmental education faculty member can share the information with the student and teach the student how to advocate on his or her own behalf.

Advising. The faculty member who assumes the role of advocate must work closely with the student's academic adviser. According to Mangrum and Strichart (1984), the adviser must control the number of courses that the student takes in a term, control the difficulty of the course load, consider the frequency and length of course settings, consider who is teaching a course, consider the instructional techniques used, encourage the student to prepare for courses in advance, and contract with the student in regard to attendance and productivity. The contract can include an agreement to attend classes regularly, to conference with the professor if the student receives a grade of C or lower, to study on a daily basis, and to meet all course requirements.

Career Counseling. Not only must services be extended within the developmental education program, they must also be extended to other departments, such as the counseling department, the vocational education department, and the adult education department. First, changes can be initiated in the counseling department, the vocational education department, or both. The counselor or vocational education teacher who becomes aware of a student's learning strengths and weaknesses may make very different career recommendations than the counselor or teacher who does not possess such information. Careers and occupations must be analyzed for task requirements in order to determine whether the learning-disabled student can be successful on the job. For example, the learning-disabled student who cannot process information auditorily may not be successful as a telephone receptionist. Or, the student who lacks spatial orientation abilities is likely to find the job of mapmaker very difficult.

Social Skills Training. Finally, the counselor or vocational educator who works with a learning-disabled student must understand that such a student often lacks the ability to make fine distinctions socially. For example, learning-disabled students may not have a good grasp of a job situation because they interpret idiomatic expressions literally. They may not understand hidden agendas or read body language or facial expressions accurately. This is not to imply that they will not be successful on the job but that they may need assistance in developing successful interpersonal relationships on the job. Courses providing such assistance to learning-disabled community college students have already been developed. For example, the Minnesota Association for Children and Adults with Learning Disabilities (1984) has developed a ten- to fifteen-hour course entitled "Good for Me" that helps students to establish the social skills needed for success on the job. The University of Kansas (1981) developed the ASSET program. This social program for adolescents consists of videocassettes and a leader's guide aimed at helping students to improve their social skills. Role playing is a critical component of this program.

The second department that must institute change if the learning-disabled student is to be served appropriately is the adult education department. Unfortunately, many learning-disabled students do not finish traditional high school programs. They opt, instead, for GED programs. Therefore, GED instructors must be aware of the educational, social, and emotional needs of learning-disabled students. It is a tragic mistake to assume that all students who seek a GED program merely need remedial instruction. Repetition and reduced rate of learning are not the most appropriate techniques for the learning-disabled student. Such techniques often lead to resentment, because they foster the development of poor self-image.

What Information Resources Are Available?

The third question of vital importance to faculty who work with learning-disabled adults is where to get help. A list of organizations, publications, and some community college programs may be beneficial.

Organizations. These organizations can provide support services to learning-disabled adults and information for the public:

LAUNCH, Inc.
The Coalition of Learning Disabled Adults
Special Education Department
East Texas State University
Binnion Hall, Room 221
Commerce, Texas 75428–1907
(214) 886-5932

Association of Learning Disabled Adults
P.O. Box 9722, Friendship Station
Washington, D.C. 20016

Council for Learning Disabilities CEC
Department of Special Education
University of Kentucky
Louisville, Kentucky 40292

Information Center for Individuals with Disabilities
20 Park Plaza, Room 330
Boston, Massachusetts 02116
(617) 727-5540

National Network of Learning Disabled Adults
P.O. Box 3130
Richardson, Texas, 75080

The Puzzle People
122 Belvedere Drive
Mill Valley, California 94941
(415) 388-4236

Time Out to Enjoy, Inc.
114 Garfield Street
Oak Park, Illinois 60304
(312) 383-9017

Closer Look Learning Disabled Teen Line
Washington, D.C.
(800) 522-3458

Publications. Several publications provide current information about learning disabilities, funding resources, and services. The Association of Handicapped Student Services Programs in Postsecondary Education publishes an *Annotated Bibliography of Services and Auxiliary Aids.* Address requests to Ms. Sherry Robinson, Chairperson, Communication Committee, AHSSPPE, 12000 S.W. 49th Street, Portland, Oregon 47219; (503) 244-6111, ext. 339. Project HEATH (Higher Education and the Handicapped) publishes a news bulletin, fact sheets, and a resource directory. For more information, contact Ms. Rhonda C. Hartman, Director, Project HEATH Resource Center, American Council on Education, One Dupont Circle, N.W., Washington, D.C. 20036; (202) 833-4707. *Campus Access for Learning Disabled Students* by Barbara Scheiber and Jeanne Talpers, a handbook that focuses on the selection of postsecondary programs, is available for $17.95 prepaid from Closer Look, 1201 16th Street, N.W., Washington, D.C. 20036. Time Out to Enjoy, Inc. publishes *A Guide to Postsecondary Educational Opportunities for the Learning Disabled,* by Diane M. Ridenous and Jane Johnston. For more information, contact the organization at the address given in the preceding section. Finally, *The College Student with a Learning Disability* is available for $2.50 prepaid from the Association for Children and Adults with Learning Disabilities, 4156 Library Road, Pittsburgh, Pennsylvania 15234.

Postsecondary Programs. The reader should also be aware of the many ERIC documents and journal articles that describe two-year college programs for learning-disabled students. The ERIC data base includes descriptions of programs at King Edward Campus, Nova Scotia (Cant and others, 1980); Kingsborough Community College, New York (Siegel, 1979); the Los Angeles Community College District, California (Schmoeller and Kester, 1977); the Minnesota Community Colleges (Ugland and Duane, 1976); Mitchell College, Connecticut (McGuire and others, 1984); Mt. San Antonio College, California (Andrews and Gregoire, 1982); Normandale Community College, Minnesota (Hanson, 1983); Orange Coast College, California (Spear, 1979); Queensborough Community College, New York (Bergman, 1978); San Diego Mesa College, California (Anderson and others, 1981); Ventura College, California (Barsch, 1980); and West Valley College, California (Tuscher and others, 1977). Additional ERIC documents on related topics are cited in Chapter Nine of this volume.

Conclusion

This chapter has addressed the issue of serving the needs of the adult learning-disabled population within the community college setting. Such students represent a new challenge for developmental education programs across the nation. Although the challenge is great, the promise is greater still. Lawrence, Kent, and Henson (1982, p. 164) perhaps say it best: "Give the disabled access to colleges and universities, and they will match the nondisabled in their performance, progress, and promise."

References

Algozzine, B., and Ysseldyke, J. "Learning Disabilities as a Subset of School Failure: The Oversophistication of a Concept." *Exceptional Children*, 1983, *50*, 242–246.

Alley, G., and Deshler, D. *Teaching the Learning-Disabled Adolescent: Strategies and Methods*. Denver, Colo.: Love Publishing, 1979.

Anderson, W. R., and others. *Federally Funded Programs for Disabled Students: Models for Postsecondary Campuses. A Summary of Regional Education Programs, 1975–1980*. Washington, D.C.: HEATH/Closer Look Resource Center, American Council on Education, 1981. 115 pp. (ED 208 796)

Andrews, J. E., and Gregoire, E. "A Study of Student Performance in Learning Disabilities Program at Mt. San Antonio College: Learning Theory." Unpublished doctoral practicum, Nova University, 1982. 18 pp. (ED 240 753)

Association for Children and Adults with Learning Disabilities. "Vocational Committee Survey." *ACLD Newsbriefs*, 1982, *145*, 20–33.

Association for Children and Adults with Learning Disabilities. "Resolution on Learning Disabilities as a Lifelong Condition." Floor resolution of the Annual International Conference of the Association for Children and Adults with Learning Disabilities, New Orleans, La., February 28–March 2, 1984.

Barsch, J. "Community College: New Opportunities for the Learning-Disabled Student." *Academic Therapy*, 1980, *15*, 467–470.

Benton, A. L. *Benton Visual Retention Test*. New York: Psychological Corp., 1956.

Bergman, I. B. "A Learning Clinic Where All Participants Learn." Unpublished report, 1978. 16 pp. (ED 181 992)

Brigance, A. H. *Brigance Diagnostic Inventory of Essential Skills*. North Billerica, Mass.: Curriculum Associates, 1981.

Cant, M. J., and others. *The Individualized Educational Program for Learning-Disabled Adults*. Vancouver, B.C.: Vancouver Community College, 1980. 37 pp. (ED 192 491)

Chalfant, J. C. "Identifying Learning-Disabled Students: A Summary of the National Task Force Report." *Learning Disabilities Focus*, 1985, *1* (1), 9–20.

Connolly, A. J., Nachtman, W., and Pritchett, E. M. *Keymath Diagnostic Arithmetic Test*. Circle Pines, Minn.: American Guidance Services, 1976.

Dunn, K., Dunn, R., and Price, G. E. *Learning Styles Inventory*. Lawrence, Kan.: Price Systems, 1985.

Dunn, L., and Dunn, L. *Peabody Picture Vocabulary Test, Revised*. Circle Pines, Minn.: American Guidance Services, 1981.

Goldman, R., Fristoe, M., and Woodcock, R. *Goldman-Fristoe-Woodcock Auditory Skills Test Battery*. Circle Pines, Minn.: American Guidance Services, 1974.

Hammill, D. D. *Detroit Tests of Learning Aptitude, Revised*. Austin, Tex.: Services for Professional Educators, 1985.

Hammill, D. D., and Larsen, S. C. *Test of Written Language.* Austin, Tex.: Services for Professional Educators, 1978.

Hammill, D. D., Leigh, J. E., McNutt, G., and Larsen, S. C. "A New Definition of Learning Disabilities." *Learning Disability Quarterly,* 1981, *4,* 336–342.

Hanson, K. M. *A Comprehensive Program for Handicapped Students at the Two-Year College.* Bloomington, Minn.: Normandale Community College, 1983. 73 pp. (ED 230 233)

Hill, J. "Cognitive Style Interest Inventory." In *Personalized Education Programs Utilizing Cognitive Style Mapping.* Bloomfield Hills, Mich.: Oakland Community College, 1971.

Keogh, B. K., Major-Kingsley, S., Omori-Gordon, H., and Reid, H. P. *A System of Marker Variables for the Field of Learning Disabilities.* Syracuse, N.Y.: Syracuse University Press, 1982.

Kirk, S. A. *Special Education for Handicapped Children: First Annual Report of the National Advisory Committee on Handicapped Children.* Washington, D.C.: Office of Education, 1968. 55 pp. (ED 018 058)

Kolb, D. A. *Learning Style Inventory.* Boston: McBer, 1976.

Larsen, S., and Hammill, D. *Test of Written Spelling.* San Rafael, Calif.: Academic Therapy Publications, 1976.

Lerner, J. W. *Children with Learning Disabilities.* Boston: Houghton Mifflin, 1976.

Lawrence, J. K., Kent, L., and Henson, J. W. *The Handicapped Student in America's Colleges: A Longitudinal Analysis. Part 1: Disabled 1978 College Freshmen.* Los Angeles: Higher Education Research Institute, 1981. 562 pp. (ED 215 625)

Lawrence, J. K., Kent, L., and Henson, J. W. *The Handicapped Student in America's Colleges: A Longitudinal Analysis. Part 3: Disabled 1978 College Freshmen Three Years Later.* Los Angeles: Higher Education Research Institute, 1982. 249 pp. (ED 226 694)

Lyon, G. R. "Identification and Remediation of Learning Disability Subtypes: Preliminary Findings." *Learning Disabilities Focus,* 1985, *1* (1), 21–35.

McGuire, J., and others. *The Development of a Support Program for Learning-Disabled Students in a Junior College Setting.* New London, Conn.: Mitchell College, 1984. 88 pp. (ED 243 532)

Mangrum, C. T., and Strichart, S. S. *College and the Learning-Disabled Student: A Guide to Program Selection, Development, and Implementation.* New York: Grune & Stratton, 1984.

Minnesota Association for Children and Adults with Learning Disabilities. *Good for Me: A Living Skills Program.* St. Paul: Minnesota Association for Children and Adults with Learning Disabilities, 1984.

National Information Center for Handicapped Children and Youth. *News Digest.* Rosslyn, Va.: National Information Center for Handicapped Children and Youth, 1985.

New York Association for Children and Adults with Learning Disabilities. *Project Independence.* New York: New York Association for Children and Adults with Learning Disabilities, 1983.

Ostertag, B. A., and Baker, R. E. *A Follow-Up Study of Learning-Disabled Programs in California Community Colleges.* Sacramento, Calif.: Office of the Chancellor for Community Colleges, 1984.

Schmoeller, V., and Kester, D. L. *This Model Management and Evaluation System of a Large $1.5 Million Program for Handicapped Students in All Nine Los Angeles Community Colleges Provides Both Cost-Benefit Analysis and Program Quality Information.* Los Angeles: Los Angeles Community College District, 1977. 44 pp. (ED 148 451)

Shepard, L. A., Smith, M. L., and Vojir, C. P. "Characteristics of Pupils Identified as Learning Disabled." *Educational Research Quarterly*, 1983, *20*, 309–331.

Siegel, D. "Help for Learning-Disabled College Students." *American Education*, 1979, *15* (6), 17–21.

Smith-Davis, J. *When Handicapped Children Grow Up*. Rosslyn, Va.: National Information Center for Handicapped Children and Youth, 1983.

Spear, B. E. "Yes, There's Hope for Adults with Learning Disabilities." Paper presented at the International Convention of the Association for Children with Learning Disabilities, San Francisco, March 3, 1979. 51 pp. (ED 175 508)

Tuscher, M., and others. *West Valley College Comprehensive Plan for Special Education, 1977–1978*. Saratoga, Calif.: West Valley College, 1977. 71 pp. (ED 146 956)

Ugland, R. and Duane, G. *Serving Students with Specific Learning Disabilities in Higher Education: A Demonstration Project at Three Minnesota Community Colleges*. Bloomington, Minn.: Normandale Community College, 1976. 73 pp. (ED 135 434)

University of Kansas. *ASSET: A Social Skills Program for Adolescents*. Champagne, Ill.: Research Press, 1981.

Wechsler, D. *Wechsler Adult Intelligence Scale, Revised*. New York: Psychological Corp., 1981.

Wepman, J. M. *Auditory Discrimination Test, Revised*. Palm Springs, Calif.: Language Research Associates, 1975.

Wepman, J. M. *Visual Discrimination Test*. Palm Springs, Calif.: Language Research Associates, 1976a.

Wepman, J. M. *Visual Memory Test*. Palm Springs, Calif.: Language Research Associates, 1976b.

Woodcock, R. W. *Woodcock Reading Mastery Tests*. Circle Pines, Minn.: American Guidance Service, 1981.

Bonnie J. Young is professor of special education and learning disabilities at Oregon State University/Western Oregon State College School of Education.

Bonnie L. Staebler is associate professor of special education and learning disabilities at Oregon State University/Western Oregon State College School of Education.

Because the new generation of students has diverse needs,
reading should be taught in many ways.

Reading and Developmental Education

Karen S. Piepmeier

The community college student needs to be able not only to read text-books and manuals but, more important, to know how to study and remember their content. An increasing number of community college students do not have these necessary reading or study skills. Older adult students are entering community college without high school diplomas due to open-door policies (Carnegie Commission on Higher Education, 1970). Some of these students have acquired excellent reading and study skills, others have only superficial skills, and still others are unable to read even simple materials (Purvis and Niles, 1984). It has been estimated that more than 50 percent of all students entering community colleges read below the eighth-grade level and that 20 to 35 percent read at or below the fourth-grade level (Friedlander and Grede, 1981). Large numbers of adults entering community colleges can be classified as illiterate. The authors of a report on the study of literacy development in community colleges define literacy as "the ability to perform reading, writing, and figuring tasks consonant with the expectations and needs of the individual" (Roueche and Comstock, 1981, p. v). A large percentage of students in community colleges need to improve their reading and study skills. This is a problem that all community college educators need to resolve.

K. M. Ahrendt (ed.). *Teaching the Developmental Education Student.*
New Directions for Community Colleges, no. 57. San Francisco: Jossey-Bass, Spring 1987.

Formal Testing and School Records

Formal testing is not a reliable way of determining the abilities of adult students. Standardized reading tests do not measure the abilities of adult students because the results of these tests depend on speed, reading ability, acculturation, and other extraneous factors, such as anxiety level (Cross, 1981). Critics of formal testing say that the short reading passages and isolated vocabulary words found in most testing instruments are not an adequate test of reading ability (Trillin and Associates, 1980). School records, including high school grades, say nothing about the difficulty of that education or any additional maturation or experience that the student has acquired in society and the world of work. With an expanded curriculum of nontraditional courses and possible grade inflation, reading ability can no longer be assumed even when the student's grade point average is high. In addition, many industries sponsor training and specialized classes for their employees. These classes often do not carry credit, but they do provide additional skills, experience, and confidence. Discovering the strengths and weaknesses of students and meeting their needs is the responsibility of all community college instructors.

Informal Evaluation and Student Discovery

Working together, teachers and students can discover weaknesses in reading and learning skills without giving the students a sense of failure or inadequacy. Several activities can be used with little effort and great reward. These activities provide the teacher with an indication of a student's ability to succeed with the reading material used in the classroom. One such activity involves the Content Reading Inventory (Readence, Bean, and Baldwin, 1985). This inventory has three sections. Section one informally tests the student's ability to know and use the aids in a textbook and in the library. The use of such internal aids as a glossary, index, and table of contents and of such external aids as the *Reader's Guide*, the card catalogue, and encyclopedias is tested. Section two indicates the student's ability to deal with specialized and technical vocabulary. Section three examines the student's ability to understand the author's organizational structure as well as implicit and explicit text information. This activity can reveal students' specific strengths and weaknesses with all the reading material used in a course.

Another informal assessment activity involves the cloze procedure. The cloze procedure is easy to prepare and administer in the classroom, and it provides a written and scored record of a student's ability to deal with specific reading material. In the cloze procedure, a 250- to 300-word passage is selected from the beginning of the text. After the first twenty-five words, every fifth word is deleted until fifty words have been deleted. No words are deleted from the rest of the passage. Students then fill in the blanks left by the deleted words. Only exact replacements are counted as correct. Students who are able to replace between 40 and 60 percent of the words correctly indicate that they will be able to read and understand the text. Students who score below 40 percent correct may find the text or reading material too difficult. Students who score above 60 percent correct may find the text too easy. This assessment activity encourages students to predict word meanings. It also enables instructors to plan instruction based on students' reading levels, either by choosing additional reading material that is more challenging or by providing study aids in the classroom (Readence, Bean, and Baldwin, 1985). The cloze procedure should not be assumed to be directly associated with comprehension. Use of the cloze procedure to assess comprehension depends on the reader's purpose, the demands of the text, and the instructor's follow-up during and after a cloze activity (Tierney, Readence, and Dishner, 1985). The maze technique is another option for estimating a student's reading skills. This technique differs from the cloze procedure by offering three choices for each blank space in the reading passage. These two activities provide the teacher with information not only about the student but also about the value of the textbook or reading materials (Vacca and Vacca, 1986). In addition, by using material from later chapters, these activities can be used as classroom activities to encourage prediction. There is very little research that supports the use of the cloze procedure either for testing or for the development of comprehension (Tierney, Readence, and Dishner, 1985).

Whatever the etiology of poor student skills, it is necessary for community college and developmental education teachers to help students to see the connection between good study skills and success in learning. If a student is not a successful learner because he or she lacks study skills, the student needs to have access to strategies that will focus his or her attention on selected aspects of text, provide a format for organizing text, and facilitate his or her attempts to practice and use the materials of a specific content area. Formula techniques for studying, such as Robinson's SQ3R, help students to understand that effective studying is a planned process. SQ3R stands for *survey, question, read, recite,* and *review.* The student can use these words as cues to remember study techniques. First, the student skims over the text or reading material. Then, the student turns the headings into questions. Next, the student reads the assigned material and looks for the answers to the questions. Finally, the student reviews the questions and answers that he or she has written down (Askov and Kamm, 1982). There are several other formula techniques for studying, including REAP (*read, encode, annotate,* and *ponder*) (Tierney, Readence, and Dishner, 1985) and OK5R (*overview, key ideas, read, record, recite, review,* and *reflect*) (Pauk, 1974). Formula techniques need explanation and practice in order for students to appreciate how they can be useful when reading and learning content material.

Outlining can be another study strategy. The main concepts or ideas and the supporting details can be arranged in the traditional manner, with Roman numerals used for the main ideas and letters for the supporting details. Less traditional ways of outlining can also be presented. The herringbone outline places the main ideas on a horizontal line, with answers to the questions Who? What? When? Where? How? and Why? on lines that angle off from the horizontal. Free-form outlines—placing the most important concept in a circle in the middle of the paper and the supporting ideas in circles around the main circle—are another way of having the student think about the material that is being read and organize it in a framework (Tierney, Readence, and Dishner, 1985). Summary writing can also help students to see whether they understand what they read. In the summary writing strategy, the student reads a paragraph and then writes a sentence that paraphrases its content. The resulting notes can be used to review the materials. Graphic organizers and visual reading guides (VRGs) are other means of helping developmental education students to see the organization of textual material graphically.

Text Organization

The organization of a content area textbook can best be perceived and explained by content area instructors. They have the expertise to anticipate the unfamiliar concepts and terms and the particular style of writing found in content area textbooks. Therefore, the content area instructor can enable students to find meaning in their reading by helping them to find order and structure. Order and structure can be seen in the basic patterns of organization in a textbook. According to Vacca and Vacca (1986), there are five predominant patterns of organization: time order, enumeration, problem-solution, compare-and-contrast, and cause and effect. These patterns are found in most texts and other content area reading materials. The instructor can identify them in an overview of the text at the beginning of the year or as the patterns appear in the reading. Reference skills can be taught by showing students how to use textbook glossaries, indexes, and tables of contents as well as specialized handbooks, workbooks, and technical dictionaries. Having content area–specific reference books in the classroom and using them gives students practice in looking for meaning in other sources. Working with maps and charts in class teaches students the skills that they need in order to use those aids when they are included in reading material.

Reading and Comprehension

The information that the student learns in the classroom is more meaningful than the sterile material that often is presented in a reading or developmental education class. Students at the community college level are in a classroom to learn subject matter that will help them in their work, give them enjoyment, or enable them to continue their education, not, like younger students, to take courses that they consider valueless. The textbook and reading materials used in subject matter classes are written to provide these adult learners with information. The reading material is a tool for learning only if the student is able to find the meaning in it. The instructor is the most important factor in helping the adult learner (Ahrendt, 1975). The instructor can help students to use their past experiences to understand the material in the text. Brainstorming in class to discover the material that students already know and connecting the new material encountered in texts and lectures to the student's own schema are two classroom strategies that can be used to help students find meaning in their text by relating known, past experiences and learning to the unknown and unfamiliar.

Another strategy for developing comprehension is to translate Bloom's six levels of learning into teacher objectives that can be used to question students about what they learn from their reading. These questions can be presented in the form of a study guide distributed before the reading, or they can be used as discussion questions afterward in class. Herber (1978) and Vacca and Vacca (1986), among others, suggest using three-level study guides. Encouraging students to ask these different levels of questions as they read helps to increase their learning and understanding of the author's meaning.

In his book *Reading Without Nonsense,* Smith (1978, p. 85) describes the process of reading as predicting what the author's message is from what is already known: "Prediction is asking questions, and comprehension is getting these questions answered." Smith believes that each student has a theory of what the world is in his or her head and that this theory is the student's basis for learning. Therefore, when an instructor asks questions, he or she should structure the questions so as to help students to bridge the gap between the known and the unknown and so as to help them fit what they read into their theory or perception of the world. "Teachers often regard comprehension as the result of learning rather than the basis for making sense of anything" (Smith, 1978, p. 86).

Linguistic Approach

Linguists study a language in order to explain how it works, how it uses distinct units in order to achieve a communication function. The linguist analyzes language and identifies the parts of language in order to construct a model. The linguist's model can be used to examine the structure of the language, to find the norm, and to compare the deviations.

Language is a system of syntactic, semantic, and phonological parts. The phonological part is how the language is put into sounds; the syntactic part is how these sounds, as words, are formed into sentences; and the semantic part is how meanings are attached to these words. Simple sentences or phrases are the "kernel of basic sentences (simple, declarative, active, with no complex verb or noun phrases), deriving all other sentences from these (more properly from the strings that underlie them)" (Chomsky, 1975, p. 106). By understanding the linguist's theory of the relationships of standard English to dialects, norms, and deviations, educators can put differences in English into proper perspective as variations within a language. When the instructor knows the correspondences between grapheme (the written sound) and phoneme (the spoken sound), he or she can help the student with a nonstandard background in English to understand the code for standard English, that is, to see the differences and similarities (Goodman and Fleming, 1968). "Goodman defines reading as a process of selecting graphic cues that signal meaning, much as listening is a process of selecting auditory cues for meaning" (Hittleman, 1978, p. 72). Reading aloud from the text enables the student with nonstandard English to hear the differences in language and to match the language that he or she hears with the language that he or she sees. Smith (1978, p. 159) summarizes the principle succinctly: "People from different geographical regions of the country may speak quite differently, but this does not prevent them from comprehending the same national magazines and the same television programs. One great advantage of written language is that it cuts across so many dialects."

In the linguistic model of reading, reading is part of language learning. In language learning, speech is prior to reading, and reading is prior to writing—"not only historically but also genetically and logically" (Bolinger and Sears, 1981, p. 274). "Language is learned in the context of its use. Word meanings are built in relationship to concepts; language facilitates learning, but it is the conceptual development that creates the need for language. Without that, words are empty forms" (Purvis and Niles, 1984, p. 111). Films, field trips, and other discovery activities are all ways of providing the experiential background that students need in order to understand their reading. Words should be connected with meaning, with concepts, not just with definitions that have to be memorized. Specialized words, words that have a specific meaning in a content area, can be recognized by the words around them, by the ideas or concepts that are being explained in the text. Technical words are often italicized and defined in context in a textbook. Students need to have such signals in the text pointed out to them so that they can make sense of their reading. By showing students these methods of predicting and finding meaning, the instructor can make the material in the text easier to understand. A principle of effective vocabulary instruction is to provide direct instruction for technical words as well as for other potentially troublesome vocabulary in all content areas.

Finally, if informal testing and observation indicate that the adult student lacks the basic skills needed to understand the reading material (phonetics, basic word recognition, and simple comprehension), the community college instructor can provide direction and aid by finding resources that will help that adult learner to succeed. An atmosphere of working together toward success can ward off a sense of failure. As students discover that they need skill in reading in order to reach their goals, they become motivated to learn. Where does the instructor go to find the necessary help for students? Help has traditionally been available through special classroom presentations, adjunct classes, remedial reading or English courses, tutoring, and learning resource centers. In addition to these resources, the instructor can use special presentations in class to reinforce basic decoding skills. For example, vocabulary can be taught by explaining prefixes and suffixes that are common in the content area. Adjunct classes can be formed to provide specialized help and materials. Students can also be directed to remedial reading and English courses. However, these courses often use material that students do not use in real life and that sometimes repeat the situations that have caused failure. Learning resource centers and private tutoring in reading clinics have had some favorable results. However, more research and evaluation need to be done before we can be sure that this is the best method of teaching basic reading skills (Boylan, 1983). The instructor needs to understand the options that students have and then work with the students who need help in reading. The high-risk student who enrolls in a remedial or developmental education program learns the skills that he or she feels are important. Dropping out to find a job is not an indication that the student or the program has been a failure; rather, it is an indication of success.

Workshops or presentations at faculty meetings can provide instructors with the motivation and information that they need in order to teach content-specific reading and study skills. Time should be set aside in every course to help the student review and practice reading and study skills. Instructors can also examine various methods of testing the probable level of difficulty of the reading materials. For example, a readability formula can be used to estimate the difficulty that students may have in reading a particular text. Workshops can keep instructors up to date on services that are available for students who are having trouble reading the material required for a class. Students need to be motivated and taught the skills that they need in order to read and study effectively in an area that is safe from failure (Macrorie, 1984). Macrorie cites examples of teachers who "enable" their students to learn in an atmosphere that encourages them to achieve without the fear of failure. Students need to read, to learn to read. Instructors need to provide the direction that students need in order to understand the reading materials used in class.

Future Needs and Facilities

The many changes that are occurring in technology emphasize that adults need to be lifelong learners. The community college can meet the needs of the majority of these returning students by providing an atmosphere of failure-proof and humiliation-proof learning. For example, classes can be graded with the words *completed satisfactorily* when the student meets the instructor's criteria for passing. If the student is not able to complete a class satisfactorily, then he or she should have no record of failure on his or her transcript or report card but rather an *incomplete* that is erased from the record after a year if the work is not brought up to the instructor's standards or replaced with the course added to the student's list of satisfactorily completed courses. If the student is underprepared, there should be a nonthreatening place in which the student can receive help. Grande Prairie Regional College conducted a study of student skill levels and remediation needs (Stonehocker, 1985). After studying and visiting eleven other postsecondary institutions, the people who conducted the study recommended a skill center to help in solving student problems.

I recommend that the skill center be part of a library. If the skill center is physically connected with a library, it becomes a reading aid just like a dictionary. Students feel free to consult with reading aid staff for any and all reading needs. The skill center should contain computers and self-instructional materials, and teacher help should be available. Programs that enable students to evaluate their own skills should also be available. So should programs that teach students how to use the computer keyboard.

Assessment of students' skills should be no more threatening to them than taking a blood pressure test in a drugstore. No one except the student should know what skills the student needs to work on or what skills the student is working on in the skill center. The student's realization of his or her skill needs should motivate the student to use the instructional materials that are available.

Interactive video could provide a variety of experiences and teach reading skills (Piepmeier, 1982). Computer-assisted instruction could present a nonthreatening series of lessons on basic reading skills in modular form that the student could complete and grade to monitor his or her own progress. Each lesson would present a specific reading skill, give help in answering practice questions, and direct the student to another skill lesson (Kester, 1982). There could be many lessons on the same level teaching students in different ways. Networks with other skill centers could become a source of new material and strategies. With a variety of software and reading instructors to answer questions and tutor when necessary, a variety of approaches would be available to meet most students' needs.

Faculty should take an active part in the development of video and computer programs to teach the reading skills needed in specific content areas, such as map reading in geography and chart reading in economics, as well as specialized vocabulary and technical word definitions. Reading department faculty could supervise the production, acquisition, and use of such materials, acting in an advisory capacity and preparing or adapting programs for student use. The reading faculty could also be available to provide tutoring on student request, lead support groups, conduct workshops, and provide materials that described the available services.

The skill center that I am describing would include a special section for faculty. Software, including artificial intelligence programs to make the creation of software easier, would be available for faculty. Software that measured the readability of text would also be available, so that instructors could type in sample passages and determine the approximate reading level of the reading materials that they used. Teaching strategies would also be on file. The teaching strategies software could present alternatives for teaching reading skills, such as presenting vocabulary by making crossword puzzles out of vocabulary words. The instructor would type in the words, and the program would turn them into a crossword puzzle. Much of this software is already available (Fadale and Winter, 1982). However, more good software is needed. Program screens can be designed with choice branches that allow another person to write the actual program. Some programs could be written by computer students under the direction of reading faculty.

Locating the skill center in the library would make it nonthreatening, convenient to other reference materials, and visible and available to a great number of students. Students could always bring library materials and books into the skill center that reading tutors could help them to read and understand. Finally, reading staff would be present to provide material and help students to become involved in increasing their skills, no matter what the level. Students would not have to complete lessons or choose alternative methods to learn the same skills. Further, students could check out software, computer programs, and even computers in the same way that they can already check out a book. With current technology, computers complete with monitors and disk drives are available in easy-to-carry suitcases. Community college students could check out computers and programs and work with them in the privacy of their own homes. They could share them with other family members or friends who were unable to attend school and who might need to review basic reading skills. As these potential students learned how to work with the computer and improve their reading skills, they could then choose to continue their education in a community college. This would give the community college yet another opportunity to serve the community. Reading should be taught in many ways to meet the needs of our new generation of students.

72

References

Ahrendt, K. *Community College Reading Programs.* Newark, Del.: International Reading Association, 1975.

Askov, E., and Kamm, K. *Study Skills in the Content Area.* Boston: Allyn & Bacon, 1982.

Bolinger, D., and Sears, D. *Aspects of Language.* New York: Harcourt Brace Jovanovich, 1981.

Boylan, H. R. *Is Developmental Education Working? An Analysis of Research.* NARDSPE Research Report No. 2. Chicago: National Association for Remedial-Developmental Studies in Postsecondary Education, 1983.

Carnegie Commission on Higher Education. *The Open-Door Colleges: Policies for Community Colleges.* New York: McGraw-Hill, 1970.

Chomsky, N. *Syntactic Structures.* The Hague: Mouton, 1975.

Cross, K. P. *Adults as Learners: Increasing Participation and Facilitating Learning.* San Francisco: Jossey-Bass, 1981.

Fadale, L. M., and Winter, G. M. *Reading in Postsecondary Occupational Education: Faculty Development Resource Manual. A Supplement: Materials Developed and Used by New York State Two-Year College Staff in the Role of Faculty Trainers.* Albany: Two-Year College Development Center, State University of New York, 1982. 109 pp. (ED 223 776)

Friedlander, J., and Grede, J. *Adult Basic Education in Community College.* Junior College Resource Review. Los Angeles: ERIC Clearinghouse for Junior Colleges, 1981. 6 pp. (ED 207 649)

Goodman, K., and Fleming, J. *Psycholinguistics and the Teaching of Reading.* Newark, Del.: International Reading Association, 1968.

Herber, H. L. *Teaching Reading in Content Areas.* Englewood Cliffs, N.J.: Prentice-Hall, 1978.

Hittleman, D. *Developmental Reading: A Psycholinguistic Perspective.* Chicago: Rand McNally, 1978.

Kester, D. L. "Is Microcomputer-Assisted Basics Skills Instruction Good for Black, Disadvantaged Community College Students from Watts and Similar Communities? A Preliminary, Fall Semester 1981–82 Mini Audit Report Suggests Caution." Paper presented at the International School Psychology Colloquium, Los Angeles Southwest College, August 1982. 14 pp. (ED 219 111)

Macrorie, K. *Twenty Teachers.* New York: Oxford University Press, 1984.

Pauk, W. *How to Study in College.* Boston: Houghton Mifflin, 1974.

Piepmeier, K. "The Intelligent Videodisc." *Interchange: The Oregon Educational Association Quarterly,* 1982, *11* (4) (entire issue).

Purvis, and Niles, O. (eds.). *Becoming Readers in a Complex Society: Eighty-third Yearbook of the National Society for the Study of Education.* Chicago: University of Chicago Press, 1984.

Readence, J., Bean, T., and Baldwin, R. S. *Content Area Reading: An Integrated Approach.* Dubuque, Iowa: Kendall/Hunt, 1985.

Roueche, S. D., and Comstock, V. N. *A Report on Theory and Method for the Study of Literacy Development in Community Colleges.* Austin: Department of Educational Administration, University of Texas, 1981. 505 pp. (ED 221 161)

Smith, F. *Reading Without Nonsense.* New York: Teachers College Press, 1978.

Stonehocker, L. *Institutional Response to Student Skill Needs at Grande Prairie Regional College.* Alberta, Canada: Grande Prairie Regional College, 1985. 269 pp. (ED 275 489)

Tierney, R., Readence, J., and Dishner, E. *Reading Strategies and Practices: A Compendium.* Newton, Mass.: Allyn & Bacon, 1985.

Trillin, A. S., and Associates. *Teaching Basic Skills in College: A Guide to Objectives, Skills Assessment, Course Content, Teaching Methods, Support Services, and Administration.* San Francisco: Jossey-Bass, 1980.

Vacca, R., and Vacca, J. *Content Area Reading.* Boston: Little, Brown, 1986.

Karen S. Piepmeier is an instructor in the reading department at Oregon State University, Corvallis.

*The current community college focus on basic communication,
arithmetic, and study skills for the developmental education
student is insufficient. To function in modern society, all
citizens need to understand basic science concepts.*

Science and
Developmental Education

Gene F. Craven

> *"Science is difficult for me."*
> *"I didn't take science in high school."*
> *"I've never understood science."*
> *"I'm not good in math."*

You probably recognize these statements as typical of college and university
majors who have had an opportunity to express themselves on their first
day in a science course. When asked why they are taking the course, their
response is likely to be "Because science is required in my program" or "I
need it to graduate." These statements reveal a perceived lack of confidence
in the ability to succeed in science. If failure occurs, the learner probably
rationalizes that he or she knew all along that success was not possible.

The fear of failure in science that is common among nonscience
majors is amplified for developmental learners, who are likely to be reentering the science classroom. Developmental learners often lack basic skills
in reading, writing, and arithmetic. They may not have had the ability or
they may not have received the instruction that would have enabled them
to continue with their schooling. They are not likely to have maintained
the study skills that they once possessed. Now, they are reentering a world
in which they have not succeeded. Fear of failure is to be expected.

K. M. Ahrendt (ed.). *Teaching the Developmental Education Student.*
New Directions for Community Colleges, no. 57. San Francisco: Jossey-Bass, Spring 1987.

This chapter will focus on four issues: first, the characteristics of developmental learners that may cause them to have an abnormal amount of difficulty in understanding science concepts; second, what research says about learning and teaching science effectively; third, things that can be done to help developmental learners to succeed in regular science classes; fourth, ways in which science instruction can be individualized so as to meet the academic needs of developmental learners.

The Problem

Development has been defined (Houston, 1984, p. 69) as "progression from earlier to later stages of growth or organization including . . . gradual realization of potential." This definition is consistent with Abraham Maslow's theory that unsatisfied human needs create tensions that direct behavior toward goals that the individual perceives as rewarding. The highest level in Maslow's hierarchy is the need for self-actualization, the need for creative self-expression, the need to satisfy one's curiosity, and so on.

Development of each learner's potential to its fullest is widely held to be one goal of formal education. Cross (1976) seems to concur when she calls for a shift to education based on the development of individual strengths. She assumes that everyone is in need of remediation in some areas of knowledge. From this point of view, we are all developmental education students at one time or another. Thus, many of the recommendations made in this chapter are relevant to efforts aimed at improving science education for all students.

One result of the Great Society programs undertaken during the Johnson administration was the opening of college doors to millions of nontraditional students who might otherwise have stayed away from higher education for want of ability, opportunity, or financial resources. Many of these so-called new students were high school dropouts who lacked basic communication, math, and study skills. Most had little understanding of basic concepts in any academic area, especially science. A disproportionate number of these students were from disadvantaged sectors of the population: blacks, Hispanics, Native Americans, poor whites.

The need for remedial and developmental education programs grew rapidly as two-year colleges began to implement the open-door policy, under which any student over eighteen years of age was admitted, whether he or she had a high school diploma or not (Sanchez, 1977). Traditional full-time students entering community college directly from high school accounted for only 20 percent of the enrollments (Edwards, 1980). In community colleges, it was not uncommon to find students with low ACT and SAT scores, poor writing and speaking skills, poor self-image, diffused goals, unsuccessful learning experiences, and a dislike and fear of science and mathematics (Friedlander, 1979). Studies showed that students needing remedial education comprised between one-fourth and two-thirds of each entering class (Lombardi, 1979). Many community colleges have responded by providing programs aimed at helping such students to overcome deficiencies in reading, vocabulary, writing skills, mathematics, and study skills, so that they are more likely to succeed in courses in the transfer and occupational educational programs. Few colleges provide a developmental education program in science beyond the general education science courses that typically are designed to meet general education requirements for a heterogeneous group of nonscience majors. "Regardless of how community college programs are designed, they are not sequential at all for most students who enroll in them. A sizable majority of the students do not complete planned programs. They drop in and out, changing majors, begin programs without completing them. Only a small percent of the students in community colleges stay for a second year of study" (Friedlander, 1979, p. 61).

What Characteristics of Developmental Learners Cause Them to Have Difficulty in Science?

There is increasing evidence that students who choose to study science, mathematics, and technical subjects and who succeed in these disciplines differ, as a group, from students who choose nonscience programs of study. Science and mathematics are typically taught at both the high school and college level as if the student were an abstract thinker. He or she is assumed to be able not only to understand symbols, formulas, and abstract terms but to think about the ideal case, subsystems, and hypothetical situations. These are attributes of persons at the formal operational stage of Piaget's cognitive development model.

As one matures and interacts with the environment in more complex ways, progression through Piaget's four stages of cognitive development occurs. Piaget would classify college-age students as formal operational thinkers whose reasoning is systematic and involves logically complex processes. One of the tasks typically used to obtain data from which the formal operational stage is inferred requires the subject to use proportional reasoning, a skill that is required to succeed in the typical science or mathematics course.

But, studies show that as many as 50 percent of the students matriculating at a state university may be concrete thinkers or in transition between concrete and formal thinkers (Renner and others, 1976). Other studies find that nearly two-thirds of the twenty-one- to thirty-year-olds or more than one-half of the community college students perform below the formal operational level. It is reasonable to assume that even larger proportions of the students who drop out of science and mathematics in high school are not formal thinkers. After a period of time out of school, an increasing number of these predominantly nonformal thinkers are choosing to continue their education at the community college. Thus, a mismatch between college science instruction and the student's formal thinking ability may be a major obstacle to success in science for a significant proportion of college and university nonscience majors. The impact of this mismatch must be even greater for developmental education students in traditional community college science courses.

Another research finding indicates that persons who prefer and have the greatest success in the humanities and social sciences tend to be field dependent, while those who prefer and have the greatest success in mathematics, science, and the technical areas tend to be field independent. Field dependence and field independence are extremes of the cognitive styles that can be distinguished by the length of time required to locate embedded figures in a background. Field-dependent learners have the greatest difficulty in locating embedded figures. Persons classified as field dependent exhibit a cognitive style dominated by a perception of the prevailing field as a whole. Field-dependent individuals are better able to perform tasks without regard to the prevailing field.

Witken and others (1977) profiled field-independent learners as having greater personal autonomy and succeeding at higher levels of abstraction dominated by symbolic representation. Field-dependent learners required higher levels of external guidance and tended toward lower levels of abstraction dominated by concrete representations. The implication is that field-dependent learners are more apt to succeed in science if concrete rather than abstract learning activities are provided with relatively high levels of teacher guidance.

Martens (1976) found that field dependence occurred significantly more often in samples of so-called new community college students than in samples of traditional students. New students were defined as those scoring below the 33rd percentile on national achievement tests. Traditional students were defined as those scoring above the 67th percentile on the same tests. This finding tends to confirm Cross's (1976) speculation that field-dependent individuals may be overrepresented by developmental education students. Much high school and college education is geared toward field-independent learning. When instruction is conducted in the analytic style typical of science and mathematics, cognitive mismatch may exist between science instruction and the developmental education student. These field-dependent learners may need more explicit instructions in problem-solving strategies and more exact explanations of what they are to learn and how.

What Can Be Done in the Regular Science Classroom to Meet the Needs of Developmental Learners?

An inspection of community college catalogue descriptions reveals that, with the exception of mathematics and communications, academic departments do not often provide courses designed for developmental education students. Friedlander (1979) found that a preparatory course in chemistry was offered by 26 percent of a representative national sample of community and junior colleges. Only 10 percent of these colleges offered such a course in physics or interdisciplinary natural science. Friedlander reports that the science curricula in these colleges appeared to be directed to students who were already disposed to the sciences.

Most community college instructors know that many of their students are deficient in basic mathematics and communication skills and that they do not have good study habits and skills. They should also know that a relatively large number of these students are likely to be field-dependent learners who are not at the formal operational level of cognitive development and that these attributes are likely to affect the students' ability to succeed in regular science courses.

How can this knowledge help the science instructor to meet the needs of his or her students? First, a high priority must be placed on helping the student to overcome the fear of failure. It is logical to provide field-dependent learners with a highly structured learning environment. A start can be made by providing such learners with performance indicators over relatively small segments of the textbook or unit of study. Performance indicators are statements that describe what the student is expected to be able to do in order to provide evidence that he or she has met the course objectives. It follows that items on quizzes, tests, and examinations should be consistent with performance indicator statements.

I give students in my physical science course for nonscience majors chapter study guides consisting of performance indicator statements closely correlated with textbook content. The study guides are designed to be most helpful to students with little science background who express a fear of failure in taking physical science. All students are given the option of submitting written responses to the study guide items for credit (points to be used in determining the course grade), provided that the written responses are submitted one week prior to the examination.

The amount of credit awarded is 5 percent of the possible examination score for students above the 80 percent level of mastery on the examination and 10 percent of the possible score for students who achieve below that level. Thus, the lower-achieving student can be rewarded for studying the textbook to the extent that he or she answers the study guide items. Locating the textbook information necessary to answer the items helps the student to know what the instructor considers to be important. Writing the answers should help to reinforce learning.

Students who submit responses to the study guide items one week prior to examinations on the subject matter report that doing the items helps them to understand the material and that they feel better prepared for the examinations. Students who score poorly on examinations and who do not write and submit answers to the study guide items are reminded that there are things that they can do to learn the course content and improve their test scores. Conscientious students usually take the hint. Frequent one- or two-item short quizzes on the lecture topic, with answers provided so that students can check their understanding of key ideas, can provide an internal reward for students. The quizzes can be collected and scored to provide an external reward for students who have attended the lecture and been attentive to the extent that they have correctly answered a question about the material presented.

The teaching of concepts is a high priority in any college science course. We use concepts to interpret the world that comes to us through our senses; we use concepts to build rules and laws and to understand things and events. Studies indicate that simply defining a concept is not enough to enable students to understand the concept. Furthermore, examples of the concepts are essential, and it is best to use a few well-chosen examples. Examples become increasingly effective as they differ in attributes. As soon as students understand a concept, we should ask them to distinguish it from concepts with which it might be confused, especially if the concept belongs to a family of concepts within a given area of study. An example of a family of concepts in astronomy is ellipse, eclipse, epicycle, and eccentric. Similarity in the appearance and spelling of these terms tends to confuse students. Thus, distinguishing one term from another is important in helping the learner to understand each term. Comparing and contrasting the assumptions of the heliocentric and geocentric theories can help students to develop a better concept of each and increase the permanence of students' understanding of each theory.

Demonstrations can be used to help all students understand many science concepts and provide a variety that is essential in helping students to maintain interest in a topic. However, some concepts, such as gene and atom, are hypothetical constructs for which there are no demonstrations. Connection with observable experience is made through a chain of inference. Yet, without these concepts, students cannot succeed in subjects that depend heavily on such abstractions. As many observable experiences as possible should be provided to help students understand abstract science concepts.

We know that people learn at different rates and that the students in any class have had a variety of experiences from which they have acquired various kinds of knowledge and understandings. Thus, it is valid to assume that the students in any science class fall along a continuum in their understanding of the concepts that are presented. With a relatively large number of nonformal thinkers in a typical science class, it is important to begin with demonstrations and concrete examples. A review starting with concrete experiences should be helpful to all learners. For the developmental education student who is likely not to be at the formal operational level of cognitive development, such a review is essential.

It is critical that teachers provide for reviews at the beginning and end of each lesson. According to a number of studies, reviews help students to learn what the instructor expects to be learned and increase the retention of that learning. Teachers are more effective when they use such techniques as planned repetition of important points, diagrams, and other visuals. Underlining of the important points made in lectures reminds students that those points are important. This is particularly true for developmental education students, whose learning skills are likely to be at a relatively low level.

Other studies show that the amount of time in which students are involved in learning is positively associated with measures of achievement. One effective way of involving developmental education students in learning is by providing frequent, relatively short learning tasks that the students perceive to be relevant to the content to be learned. Relatively short due dates, short assignments, prompt feedback to students concerning their success, and recommendations for the overcoming of errors have proved to be successful learning strategies for many developmental education students. Regular science classes can be structured to provide these kinds of experiences, but individualized learning strategies have been shown to be more effective in doing so.

How Can Science Courses Be Individualized to Meet the Academic Needs of Developmental Learners?

Developmental learners vary widely in their motivation to study science. Most have completed only required science courses. Few have developed successful study habits in science or in any other area. Many are school dropouts who, for a variety of reasons, have decided to continue their education at a community college. Developmental learners vary greatly in their ability to understand science instruction. Each developmental learner must overcome unique learning and science-related deficiencies in order to be successful in his or her study of science.

In 1968, Benjamin Bloom based a theory of mastery learning on work by John Carroll of Harvard University. Carroll's premise was that learners could succeed to the extent that they were provided with appropriate instruction and that they spent the amount of time needed to learn a task. Bloom reasoned that, if we could provide the time and help that students needed and if we could motivate students to use the time that was available, most could master between 75 and 85 percent of the tasks required by a regular course. Findings indicate that, when students learn 80 to 85 percent of the skills in each unit, they are most likely to show maximal positive cognitive and affective development (Block, 1971).

Bloom's research indicates that the slowest 5 percent of students requires as much as five times longer to learn material than the fastest 5 percent. Thus, individual help must be given to a variety of students at a multitude of places along the instructional continuum. The challenge to the instructor is to adjust learning time for the slower student by manipulating relevant learning variables so that the learning task will be neither prohibitively long nor exceedingly difficult. Tutorials, programmed texts, learning activity packages, teaching machines, and computer-assisted instruction have been used with varying degrees of success to provide individualized instruction. Each of these instructional techniques incorporates elements of mastery learning.

The content areas that are most compatible with mastery learning have four characteristics: They require a minimum of prior knowledge, they are learned sequentially, they emphasize convergent thinking, and they are closed (Dunkleberger and Heikkinen, 1983). Science is closed in that it possesses a finite set of ideas upon which most instructors and curriculum developers can agree. No prior knowledge of many science concepts is necessary when the concept is introduced with demonstrations of phenomena related to the concept. Demonstrations can be followed by reviews of lower-level concepts with which students are likely to be familiar. Generally accepted logical methods are typically employed to obtain the finite answers that are characteristic of science problem solving. Sequential learning is involved in developing derived science concepts, such as acceleration, weathering, and respiration, each of which is based on more basic concepts.

To implement the mastery learning concept successfully, the instructor or curriculum developer must clearly inform the student what it is that he or she is to learn to do; give the student an opportunity to practice doing whatever it is that he or she is to learn to do; provide feedback that informs the student of what he or she is doing and of things that he or she can do differently to correct errors; provide examples and practice designed to help the student correct errors; reassess achievement and recycle for remediation if needed; inform the student when the criterion level has been met; and, for the student who chooses to continue, provide a new learning task that follows logically from what he or she has just learned.

Studies show that achievement can be significantly and positively influenced through diagnostic and remedial instruction and that the magnitude of this influence can be expected to be about 0.55 standard deviation units of achievement when compared with an instructional strategy that does not employ diagnosis and remediation (Yeany and Miller, 1983). A meta-analysis of the effects of diagnostic and remedial instruction on science learning suggests that the source of the impact appears to be diagnostic feedback to the learner, not remediation (Yeany and Miller, 1983). If this analysis is correct, these data have important implications, because it is far simpler and less demanding to provide students with feedback on their successes and errors than it is to follow through with remediation cycles.

Individualized instruction tends to be more expensive than regular classroom instruction especially since the typical community college class has 25 to 30 students. Roueche and Kirk (1973) report that students in individualized instructional programs have significantly higher grades than comparable high-risk students enrolled in regular courses. However, they report that persistence in a course and academic performance drop significantly after these students leave remedial programs and enter regular college credit programs.

Individualized instruction cannot be viewed as a method of minimizing the demands placed on the instructor. If anything, the mastery learning model necessitates increased teacher commitment while changing the teacher's role from one of dispenser of information to one of helper of students. In successful mastery learning programs, students often emulate the teacher's role and begin to help and work with each other.

Interactive computer-assisted instruction has potential for reducing the demands placed on instructors by individualized instruction. The computer can inform the student clearly about what is to be learned, it can assess what the student already knows about a science topic or a skill to be learned, it can provide learning tasks that are appropriate for the student, and it can provide positive and negative examples of the concept. It can present the learner with mastery tests, inform the learner when the task has been mastered, present appropriate remedial instruction and reassessment if necessary, keep a record of learning tasks that the student has mastered, and provide the next appropriate learning task in a sequential unit of study. The learner must be attentive as he or she interacts with the computer, and studies show that learning is positively related to the extent to which the learner is attentive and involved in doing learning tasks. Also, the learner is in control and does not lose face by asking an ever-patient computer to "tell me again." Thus, computer-assisted instruction permits the learner to progress through a science unit at his or her own rate. The unit can be started or terminated at any time that the student chooses, providing that the computer and the software are available. Unfortunately, much of the software needed for effective interactive computer-assisted instruction has yet to be developed. Developing such software may involve the science teacher in a new creative instructional role.

Conclusion

Science and technology influence every aspect of our lives. In business, government, the military, occupations and professions, and the voting booth, many decisions require an understanding of science. Scientific literacy is basic for living, working, and decision making.

Developmental education students are most likely to have difficulty in finding employment because many are school dropouts, and high school graduation or its equivalent is a criterion for most jobs. Community colleges provide opportunities for the developmental education student to compensate for academic deficiencies, including inadequate preparation in the sciences.

The current community college focus on basic communication, arithmetic, and study skills for the developmental education student is appropriate and essential but insufficient. To function successfully in modern society, it is important for all citizens to understand basic science concepts and to develop basic problem-solving skills.

Science instructors who understand that developmental education students are likely to be field-dependent learners at the concrete level of cognitive development and adjust their instruction accordingly are most likely to meet the diverse academic needs of the persons whom they teach. Research findings on effective science instruction that are most relevant to the developmental education student can be applied to instructional practice at little cost. Creative use of computer-assisted instruction to meet the diverse academic needs of developmental learners can reduce the heavy demands placed by individualized instruction on science teachers. While the cost of individualized instruction is higher than that of traditional class instruction, the cost of failure to meet the science-related academic needs of a relatively large number of developmental education students in our society can be much greater.

References

Block, J. (ed.). *Mastery Learning: Theory and Practice.* New York: Holt, Rinehart & Winston, 1971.

Cross, K. P. *Accent on Learning: Improving Instruction and Reshaping the Curriculum.* San Francisco: Jossey-Bass, 1976.

Dunkleberger, G. F., and Heikkinen, H. "Mastery Learning: Implications and Practices." *Science Education,* 1983, *67,* 56.

Edwards, S. J. *Science Education in Two-Year Colleges: Earth and Space Science.* Los Angeles: ERIC Clearinghouse for Junior Colleges, University of California, 1980. 87 pp. (ED 180 535)

Friedlander, J. "The Science and Social Science Curriculum in the Two-Year College: An ERIC Review." *Community College Review,* 1979, 7 (2), 60-67.

Houston, J. E. (ed.). *Thesaurus of ERIC Descriptors.* (10th ed.) Phoenix, Ariz.: Oryx Press, 1984.

Lombardi, J. "Developmental Education: An Expanding Function—An ERIC Review." *Community College Review,* 1979, *9* (1), 65-72.

Martens, K. J. "A Descriptive Study of the Cognitive Style of Field Dependence-Independence in the New Student Population of the Community College." Unpublished Ed.D. dissertation, State University of New York, Albany, 1976. 34 pp. (ED 140 873)

Renner, J. W., and others. *Teaching and Learning with the Piaget Model.* Norman: University of Oklahoma Press, 1976.

Roueche, J. E., and Kirk, R. W. *Catching Up: Remedial Education.* San Francisco: Jossey-Bass, 1973.

Sanchez, B. *About Community College Remedial and Developmental Education: A Brief Highlighting Important Literature Since 1968 in Remedial and Developmental Education in the Community College.* Los Angeles: ERIC Clearinghouse for Junior College Information, University of California, 1977. 26 pp. (ED 142 264)

Witken, H. A., and others. "Field-Dependent and Field-Independent Cognitive Styles and Their Educational Implications." *Review of Educational Research,* 1977, *47* (1), 1-64.

Yeany, R. H., and Miller, P. A. "Effects of Diagnostic/Remedial Instruction on Science Learning: A Meta-Analysis." *Journal of Research in Science Teaching,* 1983, *20,* 19-20.

Gene F. Craven is professor of science education at Oregon State University, Corvallis.

The developmental teacher is the key to successful learning in mathematics.

Mathematics and Developmental Education

Edwin D. Strowbridge

Most developmental education students in the community college are deficient in the basic skills necessary to deal with the concepts, constructs, and language of mathematics. They tend to place little value on mathematics as a discipline, and they do not perceive it as useful to them in their daily lives or in their career goals. Developmental education students have a self-concept of failure. This concept has been developed through repeated experiences of failure in our educational system. Personal identity or self-concept is a reflection of the reinforcements that a student gets from peers, teachers, and administrators.

Developmental education students have, at best, marginal math skills. Their perception of math is affected by past experiences, and they cannot escape from the effects of past choices. Both the developmental education student and the developmental education teacher must build on the assimilated past, not on what might have been if different choices had been made. Thus, the challenge in teaching math to developmental education students is to build strong positive attitudes and to eradicate or modify negative attitudes toward math. The area of attitudes, feelings, and emotions about math is the starting point for success in the teaching of developmental math.

K. M. Ahrendt (ed.). *Teaching the Developmental Education Student.*
New Directions for Community Colleges, no. 57. San Francisco: Jossey-Bass, Spring 1987.

Addressing the Needs of Developmental Students

Students who have not been successful or who have not experienced a sense of achievement in math cannot be expected to have strong positive attitudes about the subject. Even students who have experienced success in some areas of math cannot be expected to have strong positive attitudes toward the areas in which they were not successful. Many successful students do not possess positive attitudes toward math if their experiences have been limited to computation and the solving of oral or written problems that merely restate the computational components. They have missed math's greatest challenge—thinking in mathematics, experimenting, investigating, and creating. Those who can see little or no use for math in their lives constitute another group that needs attention. Thus, an effective math program requires not only provision for meeting needs but also for diagnosing and assessing attitudes, feelings, and emotions toward mathematics.

Most of these feelings, emotions, and attitudes are intimately connected with past experiences and with the student's perception that his or her needs have or have not been met. Thus, both success and achievement are key needs. Maslow (1954) lists four general areas of need: safety, love, belonging, and self-esteem; all must be accommodated for an individual to become self-actualized.

Safety is not limited to physical safety. It encompasses freedom from the embarrassment of not knowing, of not understanding, and of having our mistakes, errors, and unsuccessful attempts at solving problems be revealed publicly. Thus, many developmental education students are reluctant to ask questions and consequently prefer to suffer in silence and ignorance.

Love and belonging may seem to be far removed from the mathematics classroom. What we must consider is that excellent learning occurs through interaction between and among individuals within a mutually respectful group. Not only are basic facts and information exchanged; they are also offered, discussed, and considered. The student who feels that he or she belongs to the group can be an active participant; feel free to offer ideas, suggestions, and possible solutions; ask questions; and through this process learn much of what we wish the student to know about the subject. The student who does not feel that he or she belongs misses these opportunities and severely limits his or her learning and understanding.

Students with high self-esteem have the confidence necessary to attack a problem with the attitude that they can ultimately expect to solve it. They are much better prepared to withstand setbacks and deal with the inevitable frustrations associated with the periods of no progress, lack of structure, and new methods and concepts than students with low self-esteem. Many students come to our classrooms with an adequate level of self-esteem. While it is our task to maintain and build adequate levels, it is imperative that we build self-esteem in those where it is low.

How does a teacher build self-esteem? There are no simple solutions. One approach concentrates on attempting to meet Maslow's basic needs, which include success, achievement, recognition, belonging, consistency, boundaries, and independence. The need to explore, investigate, discover, and create is another integral part of this set. But, perhaps the most critical need is the need to know. John Dewey was one of the first to identify mental need. Piaget reinforced this concept through his idea of disequilibrium. Jerome Bruner further reinforced the idea with his notion that the satisfaction derived from having learned is one of the most powerful motivators available to the developmental education instructor. The processes of skill building and concept development both include need as an early and integral part of each process. The need to do and the need to know must be included as a segment of this more general need. There is, then, a direct relationship between needs and basics in mathematics.

Krathwohl's taxonomy of educational objectives provides insight into five levels of attitude, feeling, and emotion and into the sequence through which these needs are learned (Krathwohl, 1969). The receiving or awareness level is characterized by a willingness to observe, listen, or realize. A willingness to engage, respond, volunteer, or practice reflects the responding level, while the continued desire to grow, prefer, and assume responsibility describes the valuing level. The two remaining levels, organization and characterization, include the forming of judgments and relating, revising, and consistency, respectively. Krathwohl's hierarchy has five sets of observable behaviors that can be used both as indicators for particular levels and as a guide for the affective skills that need to be taught and learned as part of successful progress in mathematics.

Implications for the Developmental Instructor

This discussion has some important implications for the developmental instructor. If optimum learning is to take place, attention must be paid to establishing a classroom environment that provides safety for attempts to participate in learning activities; that maintains an atmosphere of mutual respect in which an individual can feel that he or she is contributing and thus that he or she belongs; that extends the individual's self-esteem through success and achievement; that helps students to meet such needs as investigation, exploration, discovery, and knowing; and that incorporates the five levels of affective learning into the instructional program both as a means of assessing attitudes—of increasing the teacher's awareness of students' perceptions of self and mathematics—and as means of building attitudes through the skills just listed for Krathwohl's five levels. The teacher is the primary means of recognizing and addressing student attitudes. Attitudes are of critical importance, but it is only through direct action by the teacher that positive attitudes, feelings, and needs can be realized. The fact that negative attitudes can be learned as easily as positive attitudes makes the teacher's role even more significant and the teacher's responsibilities even greater.

How does the teacher build a continuous, concrete link among math content, instruction, students, and the development of attitudes? Selecting activities and materials appropriate for individual learning abilities is one obvious way. Specific strategies for maintaining and promoting this interaction, as developed by Flanders (1965), include the teacher's verbal acceptance of feelings, emotions, praise; explanation and interpretation of student contributions; appropriate questions; carefully planned lecture; and clear, succinct directions. Allen, Fortune, and Cooper (1968) list eighteen technical skills of teaching. These skills include feedback and reinforcement; establishing a set for learning; motivation; lecture; higher-order and thought-provoking questions; attending to student's questions; closure, including review, summary, and linking of new and old learning; and redirection.

Completeness of communication, sensitivity to student behavior that provides cues to attitude, and use of appropriate frames of reference are also detailed. Finally, illustrations and the use of examples are important. Examples can be either inductive or deductive in nature, but they must move from the simple to the complex, they must begin with familiar experience and knowledge, and they must relate closely both to previous learning and to the skill or concept being taught. Having students give examples of these skills or concepts and of how they are used is one productive means of checking student learning.

Nonverbal communication is another very important part of the effort involved in building and maintaining student attitudes toward mathematics. Our gestures, expressions, and movements all convey our attitudes and perceptions to students. We tell students how important we think a topic is by the amount of time that we spend on it. Our eyes and facial expressions tell students that we are interested in them and in what they are saying. We even tell them what we think of their contributions, and they read not only our interest and acceptance but also our sincerity. We can use these nonverbal behaviors and skills to make mathematics easy or impossible to learn. We can build positive attitudes toward mathematics and help individuals to learn and enjoy mathematics, or we can build negative attitudes.

The developmental math teacher must be a diagnostician. This responsibility begins at the teacher's first meeting with the student and continues throughout the association. Effective diagnosis goes far beyond noting right and wrong answers on homework and tests. It includes identifying the student's learning style and preferred mode. Thus, it must include assessment of the student's ability in both deductive and inductive reasoning and in divergent and convergent thinking. Both comprehension (basic understanding) and the capacity to apply skills and content in like situations must be addressed. Can the student read mathematics? Can the student read books on mathematics, including texts? Can the student use the processes of skill learning and concept learning to learn mathematics? Does the student possess skills of retention and transfer, and is he or she applying them consciously and efficiently? How good is the student's spatial orientation and spatial visualization? We know that these skills are tremendously important in learning math. Can the student work effectively with models and diagrams at several levels of abstraction? Can the student differentiate between and among models? Can the student integrate data derived from models? Does the student have a sensitivity to problem solving? These are only some of the questions that need to be asked and answered. The point is that the teacher needs to identify important variables that are operant in the successful learning of mathematics.

Adjusting instruction to accommodate different learning styles and modes goes far beyond changing an approach or two or including a new set of materials. The visual, auditory, kinesthetic, and tactile styles and modes have considerable implications not only for the instructional modes that we use in teaching computation skills, but also for the frames of reference, illustrations and examples, cues, and models that we use in teaching such areas as geometry and measurement. Transfer and retention are in many respects as dependent on these modes as problem-solving and thinking skills are.

For instance, visual learners are most comfortable with books and graphics. They see details. They are good with visual symbols, and they enjoy puzzles. Yet, they can have real problems with oral directions and with participating in oral class discussion. Removing visual distractions and giving one worksheet at a time are ways of promoting learning among such students. Use of visual directions, demonstrations, charts, graphics, and configuration clues assists learning. Constructing and labeling diagrams is helpful.

The auditory learner tends to be a talker, memorizes easily, performs relatively poorly on group tests, and tends to have a poor perception of time and space. Thinking out loud and oral responses help, as does pairing with a visual learner. Removing distracting noise, providing a quiet place to work, and using as few words as possible in giving instruction and examples are ways of assisting the auditory learner.

Kinesthetic learners learn by moving and touching. They enjoy doing things with their hands. They are well coordinated, and they can take things apart and put them back together. Their spatial perception is generally quite good. Manipulatives, use of number lines, and the coupling of outlining with writing are suggested for kinesthetic learners.

A student who characteristically has difficulty with such concepts as one-to-one correspondences, rote computing, and sequencing at any level may well be a tactile learner. The tactile learner needs concrete objects in order to learn and has difficulty learning abstract symbols. Diagrams and other illustrations can help this type of learner to establish associations with numbers. Labeling, visual-auditory and kinesthetic approaches, and the use of manipulatives and concrete objects for sequencing and patterning are all necessary.

Most learners use more than one mode to learn. For instance, visual learners need to hear and write what they see, auditory learners need to recognize visually and write what they hear, and kinesthetic learners tend to hear and visualize what they write. When we use the various skills of teaching, we must constantly be aware that even the best lecture may miss the visual, kinesthetic, or tactile learner. The illustrations, examples, and models that we use are critical to our students in every aspect of learning. Inappropriate models can produce inappropriate or negative attitudes and impede or even halt learning. Appropriate instruction and examples have the opposite effect.

Learning Models

The strategies, activities, and materials involved in effective learning models can bridge learning modes. These models can be concrete, representational, or abstract; verbal, auditory, kinesthetic, or tactile. Models can deal with units, one-to-one relationships, classes, or systems. They can involve change and modification, or they can represent the results of such change. Regardless of the form in which we present them, they must be carefully adapted to individual learning modes and styles.

Concrete models are especially helpful during the initial stages of learning new math skills and concepts at any level. Opportunities to manipulate, order, sequence, arrange and rearrange, construct, or see the real thing can make a confusing operation or idea much more understandable. Students also need to be able to group, classify, and form categories in order to learn math concepts. By identifying and building students' ability to find and locate, record, and discuss the major attributes of a subject or object and then differentiate between and among objects by comparing and contrasting them, we can make this categorizing task much easier. The ability to find and state patterns—the major attributes or essential elements of models—has been identified as one of the four requirements for transfer. The transition to representational models—pictures, drawings, diagrams, and formulas—that demand the ability to deal with symbols becomes much easier when relationships with concrete models are finally established. Concrete models are ideal for teaching spatial orientation (position in space) and spatial visualization (change of position in space). These two aspects of spatial perception are among the variables identified by Guilford (1967) as essential components of problem solving. Other experts in the field of learning have recognized spatial perception as a critical component of concept learning.

Representational models in the form of charts, tables, and graphs constructed by students, by the teacher, or taken from such familiar sources as current magazines and newspapers are especially well suited to establishing links between concrete models and abstractions. The process of constructing and interpreting them makes them excellent vehicles for incorporating and extending the concept-building and thinking skills described in the context of concrete models. Observing and recording, classifying and categorizing, summarizing, analyzing, and synthesizing data obtained from the models are additional thinking skills that are readily incorporated into the math learning process through the combined use of models, charts, tables, and graphs. Other thinking and problem-solving skills are easy to associate with these models: hypothesizing, predicting, estimating, making assumptions, and critical thinking, that is, making judgments based on how well something meets a set of standards. These thinking and problem-solving skills are integral parts of the transfer and retention of mathematical content and skills. Transfer helps significantly to solidify and extend the original learning, to associate two or more learnings, and to identify and label critical points and constants.

Teaching Mathematical Concepts and Skills

Models are important, but successful concept development in mathematics requires the learning of concepts to be viewed not only as a process but also as a set of skills. The first step is to establish a purpose for learning the concept. The instructor can relate the new concept to other concepts that students have learned and explain why, where, and how the new concept will be used. Relating the concept to needs taken from actual life situations is another way of establishing a purpose for learning it. The second step is to analyze the concept and identify its major attributes. Teachers can help students by pointing out the main points behind an idea and by teaching them how to recognize these characteristics from such cues as numbered sequences, bold type, underlining, and italicized words. Knowing the terminology of math is essential at this stage. The third step in learning a mathematical concept involves the use of models. The ability to use models plays a major role in determining how quickly, easily, and thoroughly a new concept will be learned. A significant part of this learning process involves spatial perception, including spatial orientation and spatial visualization. Models that move from the concrete to the representational and thence to the abstract lie at the heart of the skills needed to learn concepts. Positive models contain the attributes of the concept being learned. Negative models do not. The use of both positive and negative models allows for comparison and contrast, which promote pattern development. However, Hunter (1974) has cautioned that negative models can interfere with learning. Thus, negative models are probably best used somewhat into the learning process after the positive models have given students a grounding in the concept.

Successful learners of mathematical concepts can explain the concepts in their own words. They should be able to define, illustrate, and demonstrate. These activities help students to interpret, build, and refine the knowledge and relationships that they have established during the previous steps in the process. These activities provide some of the practice that leads to retention. The degree to which students are able to illustrate and demonstrate a concept both orally and in writing is an excellent indicator of the breadth and depth of their learning.

Application or use of a mathematical concept follows the three steps outlined by Polya (1975) for the problem-solving process and extends the student's abilities to explain and demonstrate. Performing and carefully checking each step in the solution plan; completing charts, tables, or graphs; following, organizing, and generalizing patterns; comparing predictions with actual work; solving mathematical sentences and recording results; and working out simpler but similar problems and comparing solutions are all skills of application and all part of carrying out the plan required for problem solving.

Checking results, determining the reasonableness of one's answers, and drawing conclusions are probably other parts of the application of concepts, but these skills can also be considered a transition to the final step in the process of developing mathematical concepts, that of extending the concept to new areas. Extending a concept to new areas requires the student to have developed an attitude and a knowledge of success and confidence in his or her ability to use skills and content knowledge. At this point, students should be exploring and investigating mathematical relationships among many concepts and areas of mathematics, such as geometry and algebra, basic statistics, estimation, prediction, and probability.

The Process of Teaching Mathematical Skills

The process of building a mathematical skill begins with establishing a need for that skill. As in the case of concept development, the best strategy is one that relies on students' own identification of needs. In practice, the teacher must often assume the role of explaining why and where a particular skill can be needed. The second step is to provide models. Appropriate models can immeasurably increase meaning, understanding, and learning. Special care should be taken when using problems in textbooks as models. Many authors omit steps and take it for granted that students will both notice that the steps have been omitted and understand the steps that have been omitted. These assumptions cannot be made for developmental students.

Massed practice is drill characterized by intense activity over a relatively short period of time. Massed practice is essential to learning a skill well. Care must be taken to ensure that such drill has real meaning to students and that fatigue does not set in. Since skills are in many respects conditioned responses, great care must be taken that students learn each step correctly. It is infinitely more difficult to correct a skill learned incorrectly than it is to teach the skill in the first place.

A plateau is a point in the learning process where neither speed nor accuracy appear to show any improvement. This is a time when students can easily become discouraged and give up or go on to something at which they can succeed. Students need to know that plateaus are periods during which consolidation, integration, and differentiation are taking place and that these processes will eventually lead to greater speed and accuracy. They need support and encouragement at this stage.

Spaced practice is initiated after the skill is learned. Practice periods become less intense, longer, and spread out over increasingly greater periods of time. Review and summary are important and should lead to a planned and organized skill maintenance program. Ideally, students will develop attitudes and a sense of responsibility for skill maintenance on their own. The teacher as a model can do much to encourage them to do so.

The skills need to be applied regularly and in a number of different situations. Students need to know how to modify or alter the skill to fit new circumstances, and they need to know how to transfer skill from use in number equations to problem-solving situations. This point is a major source of difficulty and frustration for many students.

Overlearning consists of repetitions of a skill after mastery has been achieved. The purpose of additional repetitions is to ensure retention. Everything from learning and using the most basic facts to applying and solving equations of varying complexity has implications for overlearning. One point to consider is that three to five repetitions can produce results equal to those achieved by twenty-five repetitions. In other words, there is a point of diminishing returns.

Finally, feedback should be used during each of the steps just outlined. Knowledge that one's responses are correct or incorrect is critical at each step of the skill-learning process.

Conclusion

The teaching of mathematics is a highly complex set of very closely integrated and interrelated variables and procedures. It should be looked on as a complete whole or unified system. A number of the major factors have been isolated from this system for the purposes of definition and description, but each factor should ultimately be thought of as operating in concert with all the others. Thus, although attitudes are critical to successful learning, they do not produce learning without a teacher who is aware of and skillfully uses the skills of teaching.

The developmental teacher is the key to successful learning in mathematics. Through use of these teaching skills, he or she helps the developmental education student to identify the essential models and other materials and skills needed to learn the concepts and skills of mathematics. The teacher who teaches the procedures needed for learning mathematical concepts and skills does the maximum to ensure successful and rewarding learning for students of mathematics. It is not a simple or easy task.

References

Allen, D., Fortune, J. C., and Cooper, J. M. *The Stanford Summer Micro Teaching Clinic*. Stanford, Calif.: Stanford University, 1968.

Flanders, N. A. *Teacher Influence, Pupil Attitudes, and Achievement*. Cooperative Research Monograph No. 12. Washington, D.C.: U.S. Government Printing Office, 1965.

Guilford, J. P. *The Nature of Human Intelligence*. New York: McGraw-Hill, 1967.

Hunter, M. *Theory into Practice: Retention*. El Segundo, Calif.: TIP Publications, 1974.

Krathwohl, D. R. (ed.). *Taxonomy of Educational Objectives: Affective Domain*. New York: McKay, 1969.

Maslow, A. H. *Motivation and Personality*. New York: Harper, 1954.

Polya, G. *How to Solve It*. Princeton, N.J.: Princeton University Press, 1975.

Edwin D. Strowbridge is chairman of the Department of Educational Foundations at Oregon State University, Corvallis.

Resources abstracted from the Educational Resources Information Center (ERIC) system provide further information on developmental education.

Sources and Information: Developmental Education at the Community College

Diane Zwemer

The annotated bibliography of ERIC documents and journal articles in this chapter represents a selection of ERIC's most recent acquisitions concerning developmental and remedial education at the two-year college. The items cited in this chapter were selected from ERIC's *Resources in Education* and *Current Index to Journals in Education*. The chapter is divided into five sections: student assessment and placement, programs and program development, instructional considerations, effectiveness of remediation, and statewide perspectives on developmental and remedial education. It concludes with information on how to obtain full-text copies of these documents.

The literature on remedial developmental education has grown considerably over the past ten years, and the items listed here are only a sample of the most recent contributions. The reader seeking further information can turn to several comprehensive texts on the subject, including the following:

Donovan, R. A., "Creating Effective Programs for Developmental Education." In W. L. Deegan, D. Tillery, and Associates, *Renewing the American Community College: Priorities and Strategies for Effective Leadership.* San Francisco: Jossey-Bass, 1985.

K. M. Ahrendt (ed.). *Teaching the Developmental Education Student.*
New Directions for Community Colleges, no. 57. San Francisco: Jossey-Bass, Spring 1987.

Maxwell, M. *Improving Student Learning Skills: A Comprehensive Guide to Successful Practices and Programs for Increasing the Performance of Underprepared Students.* San Francisco: Jossey-Bass, 1979.

Richardson, R. C., Jr., Fisk, E. C., and Okun, M. A. *Literacy in the Open-Access College.* San Francisco: Jossey-Bass, 1983.

Roueche, J. E., and Snow, J. J. *Overcoming Learning Problems: A Guide to Developmental Education in College.* San Francisco: Jossey-Bass, 1977.

Each of these texts includes extensive bibliographies. Another source of information is *Key Resources on Community Colleges: A Guide to the Field and Its Literature,* by A. M. Cohen, J. C. Palmer, and K. D. Zwemer (San Francisco: Jossey-Bass, 1986). Chapters of the *Key Resources* guide list works that have had a major impact on the field of remedial education at community colleges. Finally, the ERIC collection includes scores of additional documents and journal articles. For information on how to obtain these and other ERIC resources, call or write the ERIC Clearinghouse for Junior Colleges, 8118 Math-Sciences Building, UCLA, Los Angeles, California 90024.

Student Assessment and Placement

Boggs, G. R. *The Effect of Basic Skills Assessment on Student Achievement and Persistence at Butte College: A Research Report.* Oroville, Calif.: Butte College, 1984. 23 pp. (ED 244 686)

Examines student achievement data in an effort to measure the effectiveness of an assessment program used to place students in writing classes at Butte College (California). Notes that, although there were no significant differences in the high school grade point averages of students entering the college before and after implementation of the program, the grades earned by students at the college increased significantly after the assessment procedures were operationalized. Serves as an example of one college's effort to evaluate the impact of assessment and placement.

Borst, P. W., and Cordrey, L. J. *The Skills Prerequisite System, Fullerton College (A Six-Year Investment in People).* Fullerton, Calif.: North Orange County Community College District, 1984. 10 pp. (ED 255 247)

Describes the development, implementation, and evaluation of the Skills Prerequisite System instituted by Fullerton College (California) in an attempt to reduce withdrawal rates. Notes that the system involves mandatory assessment of skills in reading, writing, and mathematics, followed by prescriptive mandatory placement in appropriate remedial instruction before enrollment in skill-dependent, entry-level courses. Includes course descriptions and information on assessment procedures.

Callas, D. "Academic Placement Practices: An Analysis and Proposed Model." *College Teaching,* 1985, *33* (1), 27–32.

Details the procedures used by six two-year and four-year colleges within the State University of New York to identify high-risk students. Describes the operation of these practices within the academic system as well as the colleges' evaluations of student progress in remedial courses.

Hector, J. H. *Establishing Cutoff Scores for Placement in Community College Developmental Courses.* Morristown, Tenn.: Walters State Community College, 1984. 20 pp. (ED 246 934)

Describes a screening procedure implemented for entering students at Walters State Community College (Tennessee). Details the three-level system of cutoff scores used to help students interpret assessment results: STOP, indicating little chance of academic success; CAUTION, suggesting that students consider carefully their choices; and GO, indicating that students have the needed skills. Includes results of an assessment of the screening procedure and its effectivenesss in identifying students who need remediation.

Holten, V. *Skills Assessment at Victor Valley College.* Victorville, Calif.: Victor Valley Community College, 1985. 10 pp. (ED 253 278)

Describes the mandatory assessment and voluntary placement program at Victor Valley College (California). Notes that enrollment in basic reading and math courses increased by 88 percent and 124 percent, respectively, after implementation of the program. Also points out there has been an upward trend in retention but a decline in the enrollment of new students.

Rounds, J. C. *Assessment, Placement, Competency: Four Successful Community College Programs.* Marysville, Calif.: Yuba College, 1984. 41 pp. (ED 241 080)

Draws on interviews with college personnel to describe the assessment and placement programs at four California community colleges: Sacramento City College, Fullerton College, Sierra College, and Victor Valley College. Examines program administration, operation, and design and summarizes information related to testing policies, registration and assessment procedures, future directions, and reactions from counselors, students, and faculty. Notes that all four colleges rely heavily on the computer, using it to provide a prescriptive printout for students within hours of assessment.

Rounds, J. C., and Andersen, D. "Placement in Remedial College Classes: Required Versus Recommended." *Community College Review*, 1985, *13* (1), 20–27.

Reviews literature on the questionable value of remedial instruction during the 1960s and 1970s, the improvement of intake and placement procedures during the subsequent decade, and student participation in voluntary remedial programs. Cites recommendations emerging from the most recent studies of remedial instruction, and draws on this literature to note the increased use and consequences of mandatory placement and testing.

Rounds, J. C., and Andersen, D. "Registration and Assessment Procedures at Ninety-Nine California Community Colleges." Marysville, Calif.: Yuba College, 1985. 16 pp. (ED 254 292)

Surveys the registration and assessment procedures used in California's community colleges, focusing on course advising, orientation, counseling, use of computers in advising, and testing. Notes that counseling at most colleges is handled by counselors rather than by faculty and that only twenty of the ninety-nine responding institutions required testing for remediation. Serves as a descriptive analysis of procedures commonly used to advise entering students.

Santa Rosa Junior College. *DRT/ASSET/Final Grade Study: Fund for Instructional Improvement Final Report, 1983–84.* Santa Rosa, Calif.: Santa Rosa Junior College, 1984. 189 pp. (ED 253 272)

Describes a study undertaken at Santa Rosa Junior College (California) to determine how well placement tests predicted student grades in nine courses. Uses the scores of 350 student volunteers on the Diagnostic Reading Test, the American College Testing Program's ASSET test battery, and Santa Rosa Junior College's precalculus and prealgebra tests. Provides only inconclusive findings but serves as an example of one college's effort to assess the predictive validity of its placement instruments.

Schum, J. A. *Assessing and Improving Writing Placement Sample Validity: Title III Curriculum Enrichment Activity Faculty Development Project Report.* Reading, Pa.: Reading Area Community College, 1985. 86 pp. (ED 261 719)

Describes a six-year effort undertaken by the humanities faculty at Reading Area Community College (Pennsylvania) to improve the validity and reliability of the writing sample evaluation results used to counsel entering freshmen into appropriate writing classes. Examines the consistency of the evaluations and draws a profile of students with borderline writing samples in order to investigate the characteristics of these students, monitor their success in writing classes, assess their overall performance in college, and identify factors that affect their retention.

Programs and Program Development

Alvin Community College. *The Developmental Program at Alvin Community College: A Description, Revised.* Alvin, Tex.: Alvin Community College, 1984. 42 pp. (ED 248 938)

Describes the philosophy, purpose, operation, implementation, and assessment of the developmental education program at Alvin Community College (Texas). Traces the program's history and describes its target population, current organizational structure, and administrative concerns.

Chand, S. "The Impact of Developmental Education at Triton College." *Journal of Developmental Education,* 1985, *9* (1), 2–5.

Describes the developmental education program at Triton College. Includes information on student placement, courses, faculty selection, reading and writing instruction, and mathematics instruction. Examines the college's learning assistance center and its efforts in the areas of tutoring, special projects, and assistance for the disabled.

Cohen, A. M. "Mathematics Instruction at the Two-Year College: An ERIC Review." *Community College Review,* 1985, *12* (4), 54–61.

Reviews the literature on two-year college mathematics curricula and instruction. Includes information on remedial programs, college-level programs, student mathematics competencies, professional dimensions, and the future of mathematics instruction. Notes (p. 56) that "the major difference between remedial and college-level mathematics seems to be in the pattern of presentation (laboratory versus classroom) and in the staffing (a lead instructor supervising a corps of aids versus a lone instructor in a classroom)."

Flamm, A. L., and others. *Reading Area Community College Basic Skills Program Review.* Reading, Pa.: Reading Area Community College, 1984. 77 pp. (ED 251 129)

Examines basic skills programming and support services at Reading Area Community College (Pennsylvania). Includes information on the counseling and testing services that make up the college's assessment program. Profiles the college's developmental studies program in terms of purpose, funding, student flow, and major activity areas.

Hartsough, G.A.K. "Managing and Evaluating Basic Skills Programs." *Community College Review,* 1983–1984, *11* (3), 37–40.

Addresses administrative questions relating to the design of remedial programs. Focuses on factors to be considered within the areas of administrative support, organizational structure, internal program design, program testing, and program outcomes.

Joseph, N. *Integrated Language Skills: An Approach to Developmental Studies.* Lake City, Fla.: Lake City Community College, 1984. 14 pp. (ED 241 095)

Describes and evaluates a language skills program aimed at increasing the chances of academic success among remedial students. Emphasizes that the program concentrates first on developing students' speaking and listening skills before proceeding to more complex reading and writing tasks. Evaluation reveals that students who complete the language skills program and subsequently take the college's basic English course perform better on class tests than students who complete only the basic English course.

Lazdowski, W. P. "Saving Your Assets (Open-Entry/Open-Exit)." Paper presented at the Annual Conference of the Western College Reading and Learning Association, Los Angeles, March 20–23, 1986. 10 pp. (ED 270 186)

Provides information on two open-entry/open-exit developmental courses at El Paso Community College (Texas). Notes that the courses, which cover reading and study skills, were designed for students who found themselves overwhelmed in curricula for which they were poorly prepared. Outlines the sixteen modules in each course.

Leatherbarrow, R. *The Remedial English Program [and] An Outline of the Compositional Skills Taught as a Continuum Through English 111 and 112 [and] English Division Policies for English 111 and 112.* Arnold, Md.: Anne Arundel Community College, 1984. 8 pp. (ED 241 090)

Presents the goals, objectives, strategies, and content of four English division courses. Outlines course policies concerning the allotment of class time, writing assignments, grading, and referrals to the English center.

Luvaas-Briggs, L. "Integrating Basic Skills with College Content Instruction." *Journal of Developmental and Remedial Education,* 1984, 7 (2), 6–9, 31.

Describes Sacramento City College's Higher Education Learning Package (HELP), which integrates reading, writing, study skills, and content instruction within the regular classroom to improve basic skills and personal development among nontraditional, high-risk students. Considers the HELP program's team-teaching approach, the three-phase strategy used to implement the program, and the instructional materials used. Discusses student responses to the program and concludes that the integration of basic skills instruction in content area classes is preferable to separate remedial and developmental courses.

McClure, P. J. *Science Mastery: A Design for High-Risk Student Success.* Columbia, S.C.: Midlands Technical College, 1984. 9 pp. (ED 259 785)

Describes a three-phase developmental science program in which students gradually progress from developmental to college-level course work. Notes that the program begins with well-ordered, tightly structured mastery learning experiences, proceeds to more independent instruction, and concludes with mainstream class instruction supplemented by tutorial assistance. Indicates that the program has increased student success in science courses and resulted in higher persistence rates overall.

Marcotte, J. "Cincinnati Technical College Developmental Education Program." Paper presented at the Annual Conference of the National Association for Remedial/Developmental Studies in Postsecondary Education, Philadelphia, March 8–10, 1984. 49 pp. (ED 251 137)

Details the goals, objectives, and components of the developmental education program providing basic skills instruction for students who have been accepted conditionally into health, business, or engineering career programs at Cincinnati Technical College (Ohio). Cites a 90 percent success rate with students who see the program through completion and notes that, of those students, 90 percent succeed in the regular college program. Includes course outlines and grading policies.

Michels, L. *Milwaukee Area Technical College: The Crossover Program.* Milwaukee, Wis.: Department of Research, Planning, and Development, Milwaukee Area Technical College, 1986. 24 pp. (ED 270 161)

Describes and evaluates Milwaukee Area Technical College's Crossover Program, which was designed to help students with low assessment test scores improve their reading, math, and study skills. Includes information on admissions, orientation, and attendance policies as well as outcome data on retention and persistence among program students.

Schinoff, R. B. "Advisement and Counseling Challenges Facing Community College Educators: The Miami-Dade Experience." In A. S. Thurston and W. A. Robbins (eds.), *Counseling: A Crucial Function for the 1980s.* New Directions for Community Colleges, no. 43. San Francisco: Jossey-Bass, 1983. 144 pp. (ED 235 865)

Details efforts undertaken by Miami-Dade Community College to meet the counseling challenges posed by student assessment and placement. Identifies five areas in which counseling staff provide support services for developmental students: value clarification, time management, stress and anxiety reduction, goal setting and decision making, and study skills.

Wong, E. C. *A Master Plan for Developmental Education: A Proposal.* Office of Instruction Report No. 82-06. Los Angeles: Los Angeles Trade-Technical College, 1982. 69 pp. (ED 248 913)

Proposes a master plan for developmental education at Los Angeles Trade-Technical College (California) detailing program goals, components, staffing, and budget. Addresses key questions relating to developmental education, including access and mission, program and resources, and guidance and placement. Elaborates on the program's four major components: counseling, instruction, curriculum and professional development, and program evaluation.

Instructional Considerations

Bozeman, W., and Hierstein, W. J. "Using the Computer to Improve Basic Skills." Paper presented at the Annual National Convention of the American Association of Community and Junior Colleges, Orlando, Fla., April 12-16, 1986. 29 pp. (ED 269 068)

Offers information on the benefits of using computer-assisted instruction (CAI) for remedial education. Discusses the different modes and features of CAI (drill and practice, tutorial programs, simulations) and describes the funding, administration, and outcomes of the Computer-Assisted Basic Skills Project conducted by Southeastern Community College at the Iowa State Penitentiary. Concludes with a software purchase list that provides information on vendors and costs.

Jacobson, K. H., and Horner, A. M. *Notes to Teachers of Basic Writing: An Instructor's Guidebook.* Reading, Pa.: Reading Area Community College, 1983. 42 pp. (ED 250 035)
Presents basic assumptions about the teaching of developmental writing and draws on classroom experience and recent research to explore elements of the composition process. Suggests that the process of composition includes several parallel, recursive, and interactive stages.

Manikas, W. T. "Holistic Teaching." Paper presented at the Annual National Convention of the Association for the Improvement of Community College Teaching, Louisville, Ky., November 2–5, 1983. 10 pp. (ED 237 155)
Reviews recent research, particularly brain research, on how individuals learn and relates this information to the development of programs and instructional methods. Recommends that developmental programs take a holistic approach that focuses on affective-sensory development as well as on cognitive learning.

Roueche, J. E., and others. "Access with Excellence: Toward Academic Success in College." *Community College Review,* 1985, *12* (4), 4–9.
Draws on a review of major studies conducted over the past ten years to examine the strengths and weaknesses of institutional responses to the growing number of students with insufficient basic skills. Notes that the basic skills taught in remedial classes are not reinforced in the regular curriculum and that such courses are taught without reference to applications in academic or vocational settings. Concludes with an outline of the elements that have characterized successful basic skills programs.

State University of New York. *Basic Skills in Postsecondary Occupational Education: Faculty Development Resource Manual. Materials Developed and Used by New York State Two-Year College Staff in the Role of Faculty Trainers.* Albany: Two-Year College Development Center, State University of New York, 1984. 101 pp. (ED 253 269)
Describes the implementation and outcomes of a statewide faculty development effort to involve vocational instructors in the development of classroom strategies that improve student basic skills. Describes strategies developed by participating instructors in the areas of math, writing, and

career survival skills. Serves as a rare example of the participation of vocational faculty in basic skills instruction.

Totten, C. F. "Participants in Learning, Not Spectators." Paper presented at the University System of Georgia Statewide Conference on Developmental Studies, Jekyll Island, Ga., April 25-27, 1985. 13 pp. (ED 261 735)

Identifies student involvement as the most important element in successful developmental work. Recommends strategies to promote more active modes of teaching. Notes ways of encouraging students to take greater responsibility for their learning and discusses the importance of creating an environment conducive to active student participation.

Assessing Effectiveness of Remediation

Akst, G. "Reflections on Basic Math Programs in the Two-Year College." Paper presented at the Sloan Foundation Conference on New Directions in Two-Year College Mathematics, Atherton, Calif., July 11-14, 1984. 19 pp. (ED 246 925)

Reviews issues concerning basic math programs at two-year colleges. Discusses factors contributing to the growth of these programs, touches on the debate over their effectiveness, makes suggestions for improvement, and offers strategies aimed at reducing the need for such programs.

Baylis, C. A., Jr. *Summary of an Investigation into the Relative Effects on Student Performance on a "Block" Versus a "Non-Block" Scheduled Developmental Semester: Pretest-Posttest Control Group Design.* Monroeville, Pa.: Allegheny County Community College, Boyce Campus, 1983. 12 pp. (ED 244 711)

Details results of a study investigating the effect of a block-scheduled developmental semester on student academic performance. Compares pre- and post-test results, dropout and absentee rates, grade point averages, and student attitudes, anxieties, and specific learning behaviors and concludes that the block-scheduled semester is an effective strategy for increasing student success.

Belcher, M. *The Role of Development Courses in Improving CLAST Performance.* Research Report No. 85-04. Miami, Fla.: Office of Institutional Research, Miami-Dade Community College, 1985. 12 pp. (ED 267 874)

Assesses the role of developmental studies in preparing Miami-Dade Community College students for the College Level Academic Skills Test (CLAST), a basic skills tests that all students must pass before matriculating in the upper division at public universities in Florida. Concludes that the effect of developmental work on future CLAST performance varies according to the area of basic skills being considered, which suggests that developmental course work neither helped nor hindered student test results.

Butte College. *Evaluation of Remedial Programs: Pilot Study Final Report.* Oroville, Calif.: Butte College, 1985. 42 pp. (ED 263 963)

Describes a pilot study undertaken to develop and test evaluation procedures for remedial reading, English, and math programs at Butte College (California). Examines the improvement in basic skills of students enrolled in developmental reading and math classes, evaluates the success of remedial English students in subsequent courses, and reviews the success of students enrolled in remedial classes at Butte who later transferred to the California State University at Chico.

Cordrey, L. J. *Evaluation of the Skills Prerequisite System at Fullerton College (A Two-Year Follow-Up).* Fullerton, Calif.: Fullerton College, 1984. 99 pp. (ED 244 663)

Studies the impact of a mandatory assessment and placement program implemented at Fullerton College (California) to assess student skills, ameliorate skill deficiencies, and place students in classes appropriate to their level of competency. Draws on a variety of data sources to examine placement patterns, the effects of remediation on subsequent grade point average and persistence, and the frequency of misplacement (that is, erroneous placement in regular, rather than remedial, classes.)

Elderveld, P. J. "Factors Related to Success and Failure in Developmental Mathematics in the Community College." *Community/Junior College Quarterly of Research and Practice,* 1983, 7 (2), 161–174.

Studies the achievement of 513 developmental mathematics students in eight Illinois community colleges. Concludes that numerical skills, instructional method, age, self-assessment of knowledge of math ability, and attitude toward mathematics are determinants of success or failure.

Goldston, R. *Math 100 Survey, Fall 1982.* Lincroft, N.J.: Brookdale Community College, 1983. 24 pp. (ED 237 146)

Investigates factors associated with success and failure in the basic mathematics course at Brookdale Community College (New Jersey). Correlates course pass rates with data on students' sex, age, credit load, employment status, and attitude toward math. Reveals that, while a positive attitude toward mathematics correlates strongly with success, a negative attitude does not correlate strongly with failure.

Simmons, J.A.M. *Testing the Effectiveness of the One-To-One Method of Teaching Composition: Improvement of Learning in English Project.* Los Angeles, Calif.: Los Angeles Community College District, 1979. 39 pp. (ED 261 725)

Evaluates the effectiveness of the so-called Garrison method, a one-to-one method of teaching composition to students who are inexperienced in writing and who are deficient in language skills. Reveals that Garrison method students showed greater gains on pre- and posttest essay exams than control group students.

Suter, M. A. "A Comparison of Grades, GPA, and Retention of Developmental Students at Northwest Technical College." Unpublished graduate seminar paper, University of Toledo, 1983. 24 pp. (ED 254 267)

Compares the academic success of students who completed developmental education courses with the academic success of students who did not take such courses but whose placement test scores indicated that they should. Describes the study methodology, which focused on analyses of class grades, overall grade point averages, and retention rates.

Tarrant County Junior College. *An Evaluative Study of the Student Completion Rate for Mathematics 1403 (A, B, C).* Fort Worth, Tex.: South Campus, Tarrant County Junior College, 1984. 209 pp. (ED 248 911)

Analyzes curricular and instructional influences on student completion rates in a remedial mathematics program at a Texas community college district. Examines the impact of student placement scores, mode of instruction, class size, enrollment status, grades, and content being studied at the time of withdrawal.

Wilson, M. A. *Evaluation of the Solano College Writing Skills Laboratory.* Suisun City, Calif.: Solano Community College, 1984. 30 pp. (ED 254 265)

Compares the writing improvement of three student groups at Solano Community College: those enrolled in the writing skills laboratory (WSL), those enrolled in an English fundamentals class (EF), and those concurrently enrolled in both programs (WSL + EF). Reveals that the WSL and the WSL + EF students experienced the highest rate of improvement, based on an examination of writing assignments at the beginning and end of the term. Concludes that individualized laboratory instruction contributes significantly to the improvement of writing ability. Includes study recommendations, information on holistic rating criteria, and samples of student papers.

Statewide Perspectives

Carbone, G. J., and Torgerson, A. *A Learning Assistance Support System for the Washington Community College System.* Olympia: Washington State Board for Community College Education, 1983. 13 pp. (ED 246 942)

Describes the activities of Washington's statewide support system to improve the delivery of basic skills instruction at community colleges. Reviews various aspects of the project, including a computerized data base of teaching strategies and research reports, faculty workshops, statewide meetings, videotape and newsletter production, and a developmental education planning document entitled "Platform for Excellence."

Coffey, J. C. *Remedial Education in California's Public Colleges and Universities: Campus Perspectives on a Serious Problem.* Sacramento: California State Postsecondary Education Commission, 1983. 12 pp. (ED 230 227)

Reports on a series of fourteen site visits (including seven at community colleges) conducted as part of a statewide study of postsecondary remedial programs and services in California. Summarizes the responses of selected personnel at each campus on eleven issues.

Fadale, L. M., and Winter, G. M. *Assessment of Developmental Programs for Postsecondary Occupational Education Students: A Task Force Report.* Albany: Two-Year College Development Center, State University of New York, 1984. 34 pp. (ED 255 275)

Summarizes the recommendations of a task force of developmental education professionals in New York that considered issues related to the evaluation of developmental programs from a statewide perspective. Highlights the need to develop consensus on terminology; the need to deal with evaluation in the context of budgeting, student demographics, and college structure; and the need to maintain local flexibility on assessment processes.

Farland, R. W. *Remediation in the California Community Colleges: Proposals for Board Policies and Actions.* Sacramento: Office of the Chancellor, California Community Colleges, 1985. 24 pp. (ED 253 267)

Presents recommendations of the Chancellor's Task Force on Academic Quality concerning remedial offerings in California community colleges. Proposes a new definition of remedial education, characterizing it (p. 10) as "that process which is designed to assist students to attain those learning skills necessary to succeed in college transfer, certificate, or degree courses and programs." Responds to recommendations drawn up by the California Postsecondary Education Commission concerning the respective roles of each postsecondary educational segment in remediation, evaluation processes, and college relationships with adult schools.

Fauske, J. R. "Developmental Education: The Second Chance?" In Don A. Carpenter (ed.), *Focus: A Forum on Teaching and Learning in Utah Community and Technical Colleges.* Vol. 2. Salt Lake City: Utah State Board of Higher Education, 1983. 37 pp. (ED 234 840)

Defines developmental education and discusses its place in today's educational arena. Points out (p. 27) the difference between developmental education ("learning of sequentially related information") and remedial education (a "repetition of processes which were not initially successful"). Argues that developmental education at the ceiling level does not necessarily constitute duplication of effort and urges the continuation of developmental programs in Utah's institutions of higher education.

Illinois Community College Board. *Results of the Survey of Community Colleges on the Teaching of Writing: Illinois Community College Board Report to the Illinois Board of Higher Education.* Springfield: Illinois Community College Board, 1984. 12 pp. (ED 250 051)
Summarizes findings of a study conducted to determine the current status of writing instruction in Illinois community colleges. Provides information on writing courses, course placement, graduation and completion requirements, in-service training for instructors, and technical assistance.

Miami-Dade Community College. *Questions and Answers Concerning the Higher Education Provisions of the RAISE Bill (Senate Bill 357).* Miami, Fla.: Miami-Dade Community College, 1983. 14 pp. (ED 230 232)
Examines the consequences of Senate Bill 357, a comprehensive education act designed to raise educational standards in Florida. Points out that sections of the bill would have a negative impact on minorities by limiting access to higher education, eliminating funding for community college developmental education, and reducing federal financial aid to students who would enroll in developmental programs. Serves as an example of the legislative role in remedial programming.

Morante, E. A., and others. *Reports to the Board of Higher Education on the Character and Effectiveness of Remedial Programs in New Jersey Public Colleges and Universities in Fall 1981.* Trenton: New Jersey Basic Skills Council, New Jersey State Department of Higher Education, 1982. 168 pp. (ED 233 757)
Reviews the status of remedial programs in New Jersey public colleges. Presents data related to remedial course passing rates, attrition, and student performance in subsequent courses. Notes that a relatively large number of students, especially those in mathematics courses, did not complete their remedial courses and that students completing remedial courses persisted in college at the same rate as students who did not need remediation.

Piland, W. E. *Remedial Education in the States.* Normal: Illinois State University, Department of Curriculum and Instruction, 1983. 68 pp. (ED 251 160)

Surveys state directors of community colleges in an effort to collect information on state definitions of remedial education, the state mission in regard to remedial education, the types of courses that are funded as remedial classes, methods of funding, governmental agencies with authority in this area, the educational levels at which remedial education is conducted, and the present condition of remedial education in each state. Serves primarily as a descriptive analysis of the state role in remedial programming as of 1983.

University of Nevada System. *An Assessment of Developmental and Remedial Education in the University of Nevada System.* Reno: University of Nevada System, 1984. 31 pp. (ED 258 621)

Discusses trends and issues related to remedial education nationwide and presents the results of a study of developmental programs in selected Nevada universities and community colleges. Profiles enrollment, personnel, course offerings, and funding levels in Nevada developmental programs.

Woodfaulk, C. S. "An Investigation of the Current Practices for Preparing Florida Public Community College Students in Communication and Computation Skills." Unpublished graduate seminar paper, Florida State University, 1982. 26 pp. (ED 232 715)

Reviews research, planning, and legislative activities concerned with postsecondary remediation efforts in Florida, including the inclusion of remedial programs in the statewide plan for postsecondary education, the assignment of specific remediation responsibilities to Florida's public universities and community colleges, state board regulations requiring college students to complete twelve semester hours of course work in English and six hours in math successfully, and a statewide review of basic skills preparation in Florida's community colleges.

Obtaining ERIC Documents

Items cited with an ED number are ERIC documents. These documents can be viewed on microfiche at approximately 700 libraries nationwide or ordered at the cost of reproduction and mailing from the ERIC Document Reproduction Service (EDRS) in Alexandria, Virginia. Items not marked with an ED number are journal articles that must be obtained through regular library channels. For an EDRS order form and a list of the libraries in your state that have ERIC microfiche collections, write or call the ERIC Clearinghouse for Junior Colleges, 8118 Math-Sciences Building, UCLA, Los Angeles, California 90024.

Diane Zwemer is user services librarian at the ERIC Clearinghouse for Junior Colleges, University of California, Los Angeles.

Index